WEEKEND DAD

101 Wonderful Ideas for Creating Memorable Time with Your Children

Bob Hilton

PRIMA PUBLISHING

*This book is dedicated with adoring love and appreciation
to my best pal and eternal companion, Joni.
Without her help, support, and encouragement,
there would be no book. Thanks babe! I love you!*

Published by Prima Publishing, Roseville, California. Member of the Crown Publishing Group, a division of Random House, Inc., New York.

PRIMA PUBLISHING and colophon are trademarks of Random House, Inc., registered with the United States Patent and Trademark Office.

Library of Congress Cataloging-in-Publication Data
Hilton, Bob.
    Weekend dad : 101 wonderful ideas for creating memorable time with your children / Bob Hilton.
      p.   cm.
    Includes index.
    ISBN 0-7615-6362-8
    1. Family recreation. 2. Fathers. I. Title.
GV182.8.H55   2002
790.1'91—dc21   2002028536

02 03 04 05 06 HH 10 9 8 7 6 5 4 3 2 1
Printed in the United States of America

First Edition

Visit us online at www.primapublishing.com

Contents

Acknowledgments

I wish to thank my many friends throughout my life who have helped me lay the groundwork for who and what I am today. Special thanks to my dear brother, Ken, and my lifelong pal, Wayne Smith.

While the stories in this book make me look like a better father than I really am, I owe a debt of gratitude to my children for their patience in helping me grow up.

Introduction:
It's About Time!

What are the best activities for you and your children to do together? In the chapters that follow I will outline various things you might want to consider, but in all of them, there is one element more important than any other. I was at a gathering recently and decided to ask a few men and women, individually, what one activity or memory stood out about their fathers. Each story shared a common denominator. See if you can pick it up in the following excerpts:

> "My dad often took me with him when he was rounding up the cattle on our farm. He was like the original 'horse whisperer.' He knew each cow and they would come to him when he called them by name. He also let me drive the tractor, or so I thought. I'd help steer while he'd point out animals and trees and teach me all about them. It was my private time, just him and me."

> "My dad was a carpenter, and with twelve children there wasn't much individual time with him . . . but he did it. He'd have each child help him clean up or pick up. But the greatest part for me was going to school. We only had

one car, so for the twenty-minute drive each way to school, I had him all to myself, twice a day."

"He always came to pick me up after games and would take my friends and me for treats. He died when I was sixteen, but I remember that he was at all of my activities, and when I remember him, it's seeing his smile there in the stands, cheering me on."

"My dad was an accountant. Whenever we had time alone with him, he would turn whatever we were doing into a math game. He'd have me do things like guess the number of gallons we'd need at the gas station or how much the grocery bill would be when we checked out. I'm an accountant now, and I play those same types of games when I'm alone with my children."

"Dad was a true cowboy. He'd take me on outings in his truck as he worked and surveyed the land. I bring home trinkets to my children because my dad always brought home things for us from his work. The difference is he would bring home things like the rattles from a rattlesnake he had killed."

"Dad taught me how to be generous and how to work hard. Every Saturday morning, from the time I was six, he'd have one of us out in his garage working on a car, or electrical, or dry wall. He taught us self-sufficiency. But the one thing I most remember is the time I saw a lamp kit that I wanted to build. He showed me how to put it all together, but I did all the work, and he helped me wrap it as a Christmas gift for Mom. It was very special to me."

"Dad was generous. He would take my friends and me out for miniature golf or cook for us. I was talking to one of my friends recently and he started talking about my dad and his famous jellyrolls. My friends would try to see how many they could eat at one time. I miss him very much."

"My dad was awesome. There were five of us girls and we felt sorry for him that he didn't have a boy to play with, but he never complained. He would call us his 'six o'clock girls.' He would rotate, and once a week he'd wake up one of us at 6:00 A.M. and take us out for breakfast or dough-nuts before he had to go to work. I loved getting up early to be with him. As we got older, he took us on individual dates with him."

"I had a paper route and to keep me company, Dad would go on the route with me each morning. We'd talk about school, boys, religion—anything I wanted to talk about. It was great."

"I remember going on business trips with Dad. We'd leave at 5:00 in the morning, and Dad was notorious for falling asleep while he was driving. My job was to help keep him awake. It was a time of terror . . . and fun."

"I remember laughing a lot with my dad. He'd take us on dates, big ones on our birthdays. On one particular birth-day, Dad took me to see the just-released movie *Jaws*.

After the movie we went to a fancy restaurant and ordered a huge meal. As the food was being served, my stomach was churning so much from the movie that I got sick at the table, ruining our dinner and our evening, or so I thought. Dad was so sweet about it all, comforting me, letting me rest my head on his lap on the ride home. I'll never forget that as long as I live."

Did you get the common thread in those vignettes? *Time!* One-on-one time. It didn't matter *what* the fathers did, it was the time they spent with their children that mattered. As we look at different activities in this book, I will suggest what you might try with your children. You can buy, buy, buy . . . but nothing you buy can compare to precious time spent one on one, showing them that *they* are as important to you as *you* are to them.

More often than not, studies seem to be biased toward the outcome that the study funders favor. But if the results of a recent study are anywhere close to accurate, it calls for desperate measures. The study I refer to showed that although more than 80 percent of nine- to thirteen-year-old children said they wanted to spend more time with their parents, less than half of parents—primarily fathers—wanted to spend extracurricular time with their children. When pushed for a reason why, many fathers admitted they just don't know how to talk to their children and that makes them feel uncomfortable being with them for any length of time.

Thomas Holman, a professor of marriage, family, and human relations at Brigham Young University, offers the following six steps to help make this process easier for you:

1. Set aside specific time to spend one on one with each child. It may be scary at first, but I promise you, it will eventually turn into an anticipated time.

2. Interview your children. Find out what they like to do, and from this, formulate a plan for time together.

3. Do what both of you want to do. You'll find the choice of activity varies widely among children. Although one may choose biking, swimming, or the museum, another might simply want to go to the office with you and sit at your desk, twirl in your chair, feel what it's like to be you.

4. Follow through. Boy, is this one a biggie. It's easy to let things interfere, but don't. Children will offer you their complete trust—but not forever—and not if you continually fail to come through as you have promised.

5. Give your children your full attention. Talk *with* them, not at them. Don't lecture. Treat them as if you are out with your best friend . . . and if you do, you will be.

6. Show you care. Tell them that you love them with a smile on your face. Hug them. Make them feel wanted.

Professor Holman told me how he, too, needed to develop special time to spend with his own children. It turned out that while Saturdays were the best days for them, other times during the week could be used to plan what they would do on Saturdays. This planning paid off. Professor Holman related to me how a conversation with his children once turned to what they would miss most if they lost their mother. As the children talked, he decided to take a leap of faith and ask what they would miss most if he were gone. To his utter surprise and pleasure, what they said they would miss most didn't have anything to do with gifts or clothes or money. They all agreed that the thing they would miss most would be the one-on-one time they spent on Saturdays with their dad.

Use this book to plan activities with your kids . . . but also give them unconditional love *and* attention. And remember: Relax and enjoy the ride.

1

On Becoming a Dad

I can still remember, as an eight-year-old, the day I got to go with my dad on his customer calls as a meat salesman for Armour and Co. meat packing. I remember him telling me that our next call was where we'd have lunch, and we pulled up in front of a small ice-cream stand in Crowley, Louisiana. Wow! My dad was the luckiest guy in the world . . . he got to go to an ice-cream stand for his work. I vividly recall being introduced to the owner; my dad knew the *owner!* As the owner shook my hand, he told me what a great man my dad was. I already knew that—he brought me with him, didn't he? As my dad ordered our burgers and talked business with the owner, I was drawn to the huge plateglass front window. It was Louisiana hot and sticky outside, and I could see the heat vapors rising off the hood of my dad's black sales car parked in the gravel drive. Inside, the cooler unit was blowing cold air like a hurricane, fogging the lower portion of the window. Down at the bottom of the window on the little edge surrounding the glass, I discovered several small bright green frogs. They were no bigger than a large cricket, but they were the brightest green I'd ever seen. But what I found most fascinating about the frogs was that they had little suction pods on their feet, and they weren't just sitting on the window sill: They were beginning to climb up the glass itself, the little suction cups grabbing on then releasing to re-attach to another spot. I don't know how long I watched them, I don't remember eating my hamburger, I don't even remember if I got an ice cream cone or not. I really don't remember much more than what I've written here . . . except that I remember it as one of the more incredible days in my life. Discovering those beautiful, bright green frogs, meeting the *owner* of an ice cream stand . . . and being with my dad. Ah, now that's a memory.

There's absolutely no doubt about it: Being a dad is a tough assignment. Here we stand, still thinking of our dads as the adult, still feeling the kid inside us, and all of a sudden, here's some little two-legged creature hanging on our pant leg crying, "Daddy!" Talk about a shocker. When I was young, I always figured I'd be a father by the time I was twenty. I didn't become one until I was forty—and I sure see the wisdom of the Almighty in this decision. You are never fully prepared, no matter your age. There should be a class, like Berlitz, for parenting. I haven't been through that particular language course, but the idea as I understand it is to immerse yourself totally in the language you want to learn, ensconced among those who are proficient in it until you begin to speak it better, and better, and better. That's how my parenting school would work. It could also help slow population growth. My progression happened this way: I loved the idea of becoming a dad, then I became a dad and found myself frightened and insecure. Over time I have come to realize that we all do the very best we can, love our children unconditionally, and realize that—although we don't have a book to go by (until now)—neither do our children. Create your own style, your own traditions.

We need to get it straight about what this book is . . . and what it isn't. This is not just a book for divorced dads or for dads who rarely see their children. And it isn't just a book for dads who want to learn how to win science fairs or pinewood derbys. Nor is it a book that you should plan your life by. This book simply offers ideas that will help dads and children celebrate their time together, weekends or not. Inside, you'll find lots of ways to have fun together—some simple, some complicated, some brilliant (only by my standards of course), and some that, to you, are just plain stupid. The most important thing I hope you get from reading these pages is, like it or not, you as a dad will create memories for your children that will last their lifetimes. It's your choice what kind of memories they're left with. I hope this book can help you create something wonderful for your children and, in the process, for you!

It doesn't take much. We're only talking about time here. Some of the ideas in this book take a lot of time, some just a little. So modify them to work for you—or come up with your own, send them to me, and I'll write another book.

May your children have many wonderful memories with you. All they want is a little of your time.

2

The Best-Laid Plans

"You know, don't you, that we've got to get some dirt so that Boris and Natasha can hibernate?" It was my wife who uttered these words of impending doom. She was referring to our daughter's two Russian tortoises and the sign at a house about three miles from ours that offered free dirt.

You're way ahead of me, aren't you? There's nothing free about something for free.

Well, I thought, here's an activity that would allow my daughter and me to spend an afternoon together to talk about the difference between turtles and tortoises—or something. We could load up some dirt and then spend the rest of the day at the zoo.

A trip to the zoo is a slam dunk for dads who may not feel completely at ease dealing one on one with a child. Do a little research prior to your excursion and find some interesting tidbits about some of the animals at your particular zoo. You could even go by the park earlier and talk to a docent, get some brochures, or even leave a little welcome sign with your child's name on it at one of the cages as a little surprise.

Even the best-laid plans are subject to change, however, as I was about to discover. The problem with taking my daughter to the zoo was that, unbeknownst to me, she had gone to a friend's house to play. So I decided to do the dirt duty by myself. Off I went in the van with one of our county-provided wheeled garbage cans. I figured it would be perfect to hold the load of dirt and, once back at the house, I could just roll it to the backyard where it would instantly become the turtles' happy hibernation grounds.

Arriving at a stranger's home pulling a garbage can with one hand and holding a shovel in the other may have looked a bit strange, but they let me into their backyard anyway. The yard looked like a mini construction zone with rusting, dilapidated vehicles and vehicle parts along with sundry other items spread everywhere. There was an enormous hole in the ground: the source of the dirt pile. Apparently the family planned to convert the hole into a swimming pool. (Though from the look of the equipment, they had started the project eons ago—and were likely to complete it about the time *Star Trek XXXIV* premieres.)

I attacked the mountain of soil. (Tip: If you can avoid it, don't shovel dirt on a windy day. I think I ate nearly as much dirt as I shoveled.) I filled the garbage can about two-thirds full and then grabbed the handle to wheel it to the van. I could barely budge it. I did manage to get it through the gate, across the front yard, and to the street, but there was no way I could

Plan Your Zoo Day

My plans for a zoo day with my daughter didn't work out quite as I'd hoped, but with a little luck (and the right planning), a day with your child among the lions, tigers, and bears can be fun *and* educational—with an emphasis on fun. Here are some tips for planning a truly memorable trip to the zoo:

Make an animal must-see list. Find out ahead of time what your local zoo's unique or showcase animals are, discuss with your child what she wants to see most, then make a list of five or so must-see species. Depending on your child's age, you can make a game out of checking off the animals as you visit them.

Arrange a special tour. Depending on when you go, you may be able to arrange a special tour of your chosen animals' habitats led by a zoo tour guide or docent.

Give your child a roaring welcome. Make a "Welcome to our home" sign personalized for your child and hang it outside the habitat of her favorite zoo animal. (Get permission from zoo staff first.)

Let your child lead the way. This may sound obvious, but if you're like lots of dads, you may think you need to direct every moment of the trip. If your child wants to change the itinerary, take a detour, stop to rest, or get an ice-cream cone, let her!

hoist this girth of grit into the van. I quickly rethought my plan and went home to get some rope . . . and a son.

There, lounging on the family room sofa, was Son Number 3, thoroughly enjoying his relaxing Saturday, playing *Wreck-um, Kill-um, Die, Die, Die!!!* (see chapter 3, "Off to the Movies!") when in came *planus interruptus*: Dad, with a chore.

Plan Your Zoo Day (continued)

See if the zoo already has a mystery tour in place, with hints at designated spots. These are fun ways to "follow the dots" and learn about the animals.

Budget some money for the gift shop and let your kid take home a stuffed version of her favorite zoo resident.

See if there are scheduled bird shows, seal feedings, and the like.

Bring sketch pads and take a moment to draw some of the creatures. This is one cheap souvenir.

Bring the camera and get fun shots of your son posed like a monkey, elephant, or another zoo creature.

Take wet wipes! If only to please your wife, keep your kids' hands as clean as you can.

Now, here comes the best part. Despite wracking your brain to come up with great things to do with your kids on weekends (before buying this book, of course), some of the best father–kid activities just fall into your lap, or in this case, into your garbage can.

I had my son grab his Scout book with its knot-tying information while I grabbed some rope, and off we went. The plan was to open the back door of the van, push the rear bench seat forward and use the seat anchors as our points for securing the rope. Then, I pushed the garbage can forward, tilting it slightly into the rear of the van so that the wheels would roll freely, securing the rope around the handle of the garbage can. It worked.

My son sat in the back of the van to monitor the dirt-filled can as I slowly drove down the street testing our ad hoc trailer. Perfect! (Although my son kept asking if what we were doing was legal. I suggest that you check with your own attorney before attempting any of my more harebrained ideas.)

As we pulled out onto the busy four-lane street—the only direct way back to our house—I chose the center turn lane, deciding this was the safest place to drive 5 MPH while towing a rolling garbage can behind a van with its hazard lights flashing. All went well for the first mile—and then the inevitable happened. I heard a loud pop, then the scraping sound of plastic grinding against asphalt. I immediately stopped the van and jumped out as cars whizzed by on each side of us. I discovered, first, a wheeled garbage can that had caved in under the weight of the dirt; second, a son whose face had blanched white with the fear that we were soon to be arrested; and, third, the wonderful sight of a county maintenance truck pulling in behind us, lights flashing to ward away traffic. The man jumped from his truck, as unto us an angel, placing orange safety cones around our perimeter. (I've always felt, with my many close brushes with disaster, that a guardian angel watches over me. My wife, on the other hand, tends to think that my guardian angel must have a drinking problem.)

As the maintenance man pulled out some orange plastic bags and an extra shovel, my son began to laugh out loud at our plight. Then he grabbed a bag and began to shovel dirt. We both laughed as we watched the drivers checking out our misfortune, and we pitied them for missing out on all the fun we were having. We also laughed as we realized that we were now

Some Other "Fun" Chores with Dad

Dreading a trip to the dump? Is the minivan begging to be washed? Some chores (like my trip to scavenge free dirt) just aren't as much fun done alone. Although you can't always plan for them ahead of time, you can make quick work of otherwise unpleasant tasks by asking a child to help. (Hint: The older the child, the more heavy lifting he can do. Although, of course, I'm not advocating inhumane child labor here.)

Some examples of one-time, kid-friendly chores:

- Assembling prefab furniture
- Major yard cleanup
- Cleaning out closets, attic, or garage for a yard sale
- Organizing the garage or toolshed
- Building a doghouse or treehouse
- Planning and planting a vegetable garden
- Washing the dog

the cause of one of those random traffic slowdowns, the kind where you're slowly, painfully working your way forward only to discover the less-than-worthy cause. At that point the only thing you can do is let out a loud "Harrumph!" and goose the gas pedal as you speed away, showing your displeasure at being inconvenienced.

With the bags in the van, the damaged can on the maintenance truck, and the streets of the village safe again, we headed home to Boris and Natasha (the maintenance man following in his truck). We set up the now-mangled habitat and dumped the dirt back in. Then my daughter, who had just returned home, placed her creatures inside.

My son actually thanked me for asking him to help, and told me that it was one of the "funnest" experiences he'd ever had. My daughter thanked me and said she really appreciated all the work her brother and I put into this adventure. My wife thanked my son and me for *finally* picking up the dirt. But the most surprising thanks of all came from the county maintenance man. As my son and I were dumping the bags of dirt back into the garbage can, Mr. Maintenance had been chatting with my daughter. As it turns out, he had a granddaughter her age. After a short cell phone call between my daughter and his granddaughter, the girls decided to swap pets: my daughter's tortoises for his granddaughter's lizards.

I didn't even want to know how he planned to get that can of dirt home.

3

Off to the Movies!

A movie date is a quick and easy activity to put together, especially the rent-a-movie way. Done right, you can fill a whole weekend with your children. The first few hours (it will seem like a whole day) are always spent in the video store going back and forth among movie types, ratings, new or old, like this–hate that, and so on. This is particularly difficult when there is more than one child to consider. She likes the Mary Kate and Ashley twins or Barbie, he likes Jackie Chan, the other brother wants *Final Fantasy 6* (wouldn't the first one actually be the final one?), and the other brother wants the new family-oriented video game *Wreck-um, Kill-um, Die, Die, Die!!!* So, to please everyone, you let each one choose a video—yourself in-cluded—and the movie marathon is on.

Next stop, the market. Drinks, chips, dips, candy, micro-wave popcorn, pizza, Tums. When it's showtime, you'll have to draw numbers or flip coins if there are several movies to choose from, with each person deciding when you'll play his or her selection. If the video game is selected, be sure to put a limit on how long it can be played before everyone else goes ballistic. In my opinion, video games are a bit selfish because more are excluded than included in this activity. But if there are only two of you, and a video game is the activity of choice, you may decide—as you're holding a weirdly shaped piece of plastic with more dials than there are in an F-16 cockpit—that getting your butt kicked by a thirteen-year-old is as good a bonding experience as any.

But here's my favorite twist on the movie idea. Recently my wife was stuck taking a business trip over her birthday. And because my wife *loves* to celebrate her birthday, this was truly a tragic event. So I got the kids together one afternoon after school and we had a birthday party for Mom . . . without Mom. But we videotaped the entire thing as if she were there. (This was an idea we first came up with for my mother, who lives in Mississippi and doesn't get a chance to visit her grandkids as often as she would like. We had so much fun that my wife wrote an article for *Family Fun* magazine about it.)

All you need is your video camera and a tripod. If your camera has a remote start/stop control like ours, that's an added luxury. (For more practical tips on making your own family video, see "Lights, Camera, Action!" on page 14.)

We began by gathering around the piano, each of us talking directly to the camera, telling Mom how much we missed her. Then each child played his or her latest practice piece. The next party activity was a conga line through the house. I'd start and stop the movie action as we conga'ed through the living room, then popped up on the stairs, came out of the shower with towels wrapped around us, snaked our way out from under the bed covers, hopped out of the back seat of the car, and, finally, came into the kitchen breakfast bar area where we surrounded a brightly lit birthday cake loaded with far more candles than necessary. Our "Dunh, dunh, dunh, dunh, dunh, DUNH!" conga song became the "Happy Birthday" song, which we sang with all our might right into the camera lens.

The coup de grace, so to speak, came when we cut the cake, all the while telling Mom how much we missed her and wished she could be there for her party. We set a large end piece with loads of extra icing on a plate and told her it was for her, then began scarfing down our pieces of cake while we encouraged Mom to take a bite of hers: "Come on, Mom, it's your favorite: chocolate with chocolate mousse filling. It's soooooooo goooood!!! Come on, Mom, take a bite. You'll love it."

After a few more minutes of this unreasonable torture, I turned to the kids and said, "Well, I guess Mom just doesn't want any cake this year." And, allowing that we had rehearsed this bit of mischief beforehand, we all literally lunged at her slice of cake, digging, grabbing, shoving cake into our mouths while splattering cake, icing, and crumbs all over the place.

A word of caution here: If you decide that this is a crazy activity that you might like to try, be advised that the cleanup is excruciating. Colored frosting is hard to get off white counter tops and cake crumbs have a way of working their way into every little crevice.

Back to the party. I had taken the kids to a variety of "less than Macys" stores to get some gag gifts, all of which we now opened on camera for Mom. Evening in Paris perfume, plastic hair

Lights, Camera, Action!

Making a family video with one kid—or the entire family—can be great way to let loose, be creative, and act silly together. You can plan the video as a gift for Mom, the grandparents, or a family friend—or just make it for fun. If you have a digital video camera, you can even upload it to the Internet and e-mail your masterpiece to everyone you know. Editing the digital video is an activity you and a computer-savvy older child can do together, too.

Some things to consider:

Script. If you're making the video for a relative, you may want to have a script—or at least a very loose outline. This will keep your movie rolling along at a steady pace. Plan your location(s) as well as what you'll say and do on film. This is something you and your child can write together.

Lighting. If you're shooting indoors, test the "set" first to make sure the lighting is okay. Too many lights and you're likely to appear washed out or get hotspots on the screen; too few and you'll appear as dark silhouettes.

Equipment. A tripod really helps. This keeps the picture from appearing shaky—and you won't give viewers a headache by panning too quickly from side to side. A remote-controlled start/stop feature comes in handy, too.

Editing. If you're working with a traditional video camera, you'll want to "edit in the can," which means that you

rollers, clown makeup, a "Jetsons" cartoon video (a gift she actually loved, since "The Jetsons" was her favorite childhood cartoon).

All in all, we had a fabulous time making this ridiculous video filled with love for a much-missed mom. I sent the tape

Lights, Camera, Action! (continued)

should simply try to shoot your video from start to finish so that it doesn't require any editing at all. If you have a digital camera and know how to use video-editing software, you have more flexibility to create more complex movies—and you don't have to worry about "mistakes" captured on tape. Going digital will also allow you to add a title screen, credits, and other effects, like music.

The Internet has some great resources for digital video editing, equipment, and pointers. Here are some sites to start with:

- **www.about.com**
  Type *digital video editing* into the search box to retrieve a comprehensive list of resources and tips from experts.

- **www.abcdv.com**
  This digital video site has hardware and software reviews, plus links to tips for beginners and experts.

- **www.apple.com/imovie**
  If you already use a Macintosh or iMac computer, Apple's iMovie 2 software is your shortest route to becoming an amateur filmmaker.

- **www.adobe.com/products/premiere**
  For Windows users, Adobe's Premiere 6.0 is one of the most popular video-editing packages.

Viewing. This is the best part! Treat it as if you were watching a "real" video: Gather the whole family, dim the lights, make popcorn, press Play, and enjoy!

via overnight delivery so that it would arrive at her next hotel on her birthday. As we waited for our nightly call, we all hoped she would have as much fun watching our "gift" as we had planning and executing it. When the phone rang at the appointed time, I made sure the speakerphone was on so we could hear her reaction. I said hello but could only hear sounds of muffled crying on the other end—quickly dashing our joy with the thought that our gift of love had somehow hurt her feelings.

It was actually the opposite. She had watched the tape five times, laughing and crying harder each time, missing us so. When she got home we had a real birthday party with another chocolate mousse cake, but with real gifts this time . . . and we all laughed and cried as we watched the tape together.

4

It's Like Learning to Ride a Bike

One of the oldest, most time-tested (and oftentimes simply *testing*) parent-child activities is teaching a child how to ride a bike. I've been through it four times and each was as different from the others as one child is from the other. If you haven't taught a child to ride a bike, be prepared for every excuse in the world as to why it won't work—from your child. Also, invest in some really good running shoes; you'll need them.

In my case, Child Number 1 was a daredevil. His eyes flashed with excitement as I ran alongside him, doing all of the navigating and providing the power to propel the bike forward. It took him a little while to get over just watching the world whiz by at a never-before-experienced speed. (Would that it had been the only manifestation of his love of excessive speed, but no. He transferred this need for speed to cars, which is thankfully kept in check by his frequent lack of money due to the oil cartel and girls.) But he grasped the fundamentals of biking rather quickly—and the fundamentals of braking all too quickly.

Now that I had the system down, I was ready for Child Number 2. Unfortunately, he wasn't ready for me . . . even to this day. His heart was never quite into riding a bike. Now, if I could always be there to pedal so he could just sit on the handlebars and read a book, that would be cool. This guy even waited two years past the age that he was eligible for a driver's license before applying for one. (That was my first substantial evidence that he was actually an alien.) He did eventually learn to ride a bike; I did teach him. We spent an enormous amount of time on it, but let's just say that riding a bicycle wouldn't be something he'd list as one of his great loves.

Well, along came Child Number 3, and I quickly realized that I couldn't possibly predict how *this* set of lessons would go. I do have videotape of one of our lessons just prior to his taking wing on his own. I had spent a lot of time and worn out several pairs of running shoes getting to this point. I somehow knew that this would be the day, and so I brought the camera outside. After working with him for a few minutes, I grabbed the camera, pointed it in his direction, and asked him to identify the day and date, which he did. Then I announced off camera that this would be the day when he would officially learn to be an independent bike rider . . . and caught the look of fright on his face. Now, this is a really great kid who can accomplish almost everything he sets his mind to—but he needs to be prodded a bit. I encouraged him, instructed him, told him about pushing off with one foot while exerting downward pressure with the opposite foot, and that he should look up where he was going, not down at his feet or the ground. Slowly, painstakingly, over his loud protests of "I can't" came floating motion. It lasted only seconds, but I could tell he realized that what I had promised really could be true. It was a truly celebratory moment, just like when, in *Peter Pan*, the kids yell out that they can fly. I caught, on camera, a six-year-old kid grinning from handlebar to reflector as he slowly, then faster and faster, glided up and down the driveway. His "I can'ts" quickly changed to, "Hey, Dad, watch this!" as he stopped and started, stopped and started for the next twenty minutes. It was such a pleasure to see him on Christmas morning two years ago getting his first new bike after five years of hand-me-downs from his older brothers. His smile that morning was interchangeable with the one I captured on video that summer morning when he first learned that he, indeed, could fly.

And next came Number 4. She wants to do everything, and usually does. Except ride a bike. I tried and tried, and we both got very frustrated. That year for Christmas, she asked Santa for a scooter like "all the other kids were riding." My wife and I talked it over and were both concerned that if she couldn't master a bike, how could she hope to learn to balance on a scooter? So, I told my daughter no. (Actually, I haven't yet learned to say "no" to my wife or my daughter, so I once again caved in and she got her scooter. I just wanted you to think, for a moment, that I'm in charge.) Guess what? She immediately taught herself to ride the scooter. She was not only scooting around the driveway and sidewalk, but when it was time to come in for lunch or dinner, she'd bring the scooter in the house and ride it from room to room, circling the dining area and the kitchen while we were trying to serve hot dishes. She would scoot to friends' houses or take the scooter along in the

The Bicycling Lesson

Before you start, make sure the child and the bike fit each other. Arrange the bike so that one pedal is all the way down on one side and the other is all the way up. Hoist your child up on the seat, helping her balance as you have her put her feet on the pedals. The reach of the leg on the down pedal should leave the leg slightly bent to get the best pedaling action. Make sure the seat is level.

Keep in mind that "teaching" is a misnomer for the first little while. You'll actually be walking the bike while the child sits astride it, making noises like "vroom, vroom!" The next part requires some coordination on your part. Ever so slowly, begin to turn the pedals for her by bending down and rotating them with one hand as you jog alongside the bike, holding the handlebars with the other hand. This is how you show your child how the bike works. You may never find a more uncomfortable position the rest of your life—except for the next part of the lesson.

A word to the wise: Wait a while before teaching your child how to activate the brakes . . . or at least try to maintain a good sense of humor when she suddenly jams the pedals backward to test out her newfound knowledge. The problem with teaching braking techniques too early is that you're in motion, pushing the bike along at a nice clip, sweating and wondering if you're going to have a heart attack from all the exercise, praying for this part to be over when—without warning—it is. That's when the little angel suddenly jams her foot down on the pedal, bringing the bike to an immediate standstill as you continue on a forward trajectory, right into the handlebars—which in most cases will hit you right at waist level. You get my drift.

When you think your child is ready, you'll want to push fast enough so you can release the bike to let it and your child roll freely. Just make sure you are still running alongside so that you can be there to grab her if she falls.

Next, teach your child to start from a complete stop by pushing down one pedal, then the other, then slowing down and braking—and doing it all over again, and again, and again.

car so that when she slept over at a friend's house they could scoot around together. She was amazing. She was so good at it, in fact, that once she mastered the scooter, she taught herself how to ride her bicycle.

Now she and I can ride to the nearby park together, me on my twenty-year-old bike and she on the two-wheeled vehicle of her choice.

The time spent one on one teaching each child how to ride a bike has become an investment better than any stock pick I could have ever made. Over the years it has become a platform for trust and a source of many great stories. Best of all, I can still picture in my mind their faces, feel their hands holding on to mine, remember their fear (and mine) as I let them go for the first time—knowing, of course, that letting go is as much a part of a parent's life as holding on.

Don't worry about the scratches on the cars they bump against, or the shredded jeans, or even the scrapes on the hands and knees from the inevitable falls. Just remember the joy in their hearts and yours, mingled with that wistful little pang you feel as they shout, "Hey, Dad, look . . . look, I can fly!"

5

One, Two, Cha-Cha-Cha!

Is there a dad with a daughter who has never danced with her, her tiny feet on top of his, as they move around to the music? If so, that dad is missing out on one of the great treats in life. Dancing with your child can be a wonderful weekend activity together.

So, if you're ready, let's begin—a-one, a-two, a-one, two, three! But let's take it a step beyond turning on the oldies station and dancing on Dad's toes. Have you ever thought about taking a dance class with one of your children? I got a flier in the mail the other day from a dance studio offering classes for salsa, merengue, swing (West Coast and East Coast), ballroom, rumba, cha-cha, tango, and even the old standby, the foxtrot. Most cities have dance schools, professionals who offer private lessons, and classes offered through local recreation facilities. Check the yellow pages, under *Dancing*, to see what your options are, or call your city's parks and rec department for a class schedule.

Wouldn't it be neat to sign up for one of these classes with your daughter, preparing her for school or church dances so she knows how to move on the dance floor? If you've ever been to any youth dances, you probably know that there are two kinds of dance-floor action there. One is, well, none. The entire group stands around yakking, waiting for someone else to make the first move. The other kind of action you'll see involves kids jumping around like there's a scorpion in their jeans without any sense of fluidity.

I took a dance class when I was about eight years old. My mom sent me with the neighbor's daughter. She was a very good dancer, as she had been taking lessons for some time. I felt like such a schlub, but I did learn a few steps and felt more confident when I left.

During his senior year of high school our oldest son asked for dance lessons for his birthday so that he and his girlfriend would know some steps at the school dances. He'll never star in any dance movies, but he did look pretty cool strutting through a few West Coast swing moves . . . beaming with every turn.

To get started, sit down with your daughter and watch some classic dance movies with Fred Astaire and Ginger Rogers. *Top Hat* is one of my favorites. Or check out Gene Kelly, Debbie Reynolds, and Donald O'Connor in one of the truly great movies, *Singin' in the Rain*. And believe it or not, there is some great father-daughter dancing in the movie *Annie*. Hit your favorite Internet search site, type in *dance movies*, and you'll get a long list of good ones. (If you don't have a favorite search site, try Google, www.google.com.)

Two Left Feet

For kids who are rhythmically challenged, there are a few ways you can get them involved in shows without pressuring them to dance. You can have them help with decorations and refreshments at community or church events. These are great moments to teach them how to be social and helpful at the same time. Some kids will *never* be inclined to dance, so let them learn to be the emcee or disc jockey at dances. This will help build their confidence and quite possibly make them very popular, giving them the drive to learn to dance with that cute guy or gal that's been flirting with the D.J.

If the thought of dancing makes you nervous because, say, you're not blessed with a lot of rhythm or you're unsure of your abilities, check out the Japanese movie *Shall We Dance?* It's the story of a guy with a boring job who changes his life through dancing. It's a terrific movie.

West Side Story is another great movie to watch with the kids, both for the story and for the dance scenes. I first saw it when I was in the Navy. When I got out and moved back to my hometown, I joined a community theatre group. After repeatedly mentioning to the director how much I loved this musical, she announced that our next production would be . . . *West Side Story*. And she wanted me to play the part of Tony. I was flabbergasted. I knew I had oversold myself because there was no way I could hit those high tenor notes. So I ended up with the part of Riff, the leader of the Jets. We found a nice but slightly older man to play the part of young Tony. The remainder of the cast was made up of high school students. As it turned out, all the Jets were short, except me, and when my character died onstage, it took most of them to cart me off, dragging me rather than carrying me aloft, as the audience chuckled through this normally sad scene. Ah, show biz!

Of course, you don't have to star in a musical production to dance with your daughter. Think about it: dancing with your daughter at her wedding, gliding across the floor hand in hand, waltzing her into the loving arms of her groom. Be her dance partner now and you'll be her dance partner forever. She may dance with others, but there'll never be another man who will hold her as tenderly and lovingly as her dad.

Let the magic and the music begin.

6

Get Your (Cycling) Kicks on Route 66

So you've taught your child how to ride a bike. Now it's time to share with him the fun of a bike *adventure*. I'm lucky to live in a city with lots of bike trails and weather that cooperates 90 percent of the year. Your community may not have many bike trails, but roads work just as well *if* you follow the two main rules of biking:

Rule Number 1: Operate under the same rules as you would if you were driving a car.

Rule Number 2: In the event of an unfortunate meeting between automobile and bicycle, the automobile *always* wins.

A bike trip can be as short or as long as you and your children are prepared for it to be. Your first "adventure" could be just around the block and back. The next, down to the park and back. If you decide that a full-blown bike adventure is something you and your kids would like to do together, that's when the serious planning comes in to play.

Take, for example, the "century"—that is, a 100-mile bike trip. Bringing children on a trip like this means there is a lot to consider. First, there are the itinerary and expense of the trip. Unless you, the kids, and anyone else who might be a part of the trip are in racing shape, you'll probably need to plan at least one overnight stop. On the century we did along the Pacific Coast Highway, from Santa Barbara to Malibu, our group booked motel stays for two nights, beginning our ride after school on Friday and ending it Sunday morning in time to get to church. We arrived at the first motel late in the afternoon, checked in, grabbed a quick bite at the restaurant, and then made sure our bikes and other equipment were ready to hit the road. After everything checked out—Snickers bars, trail mix, and water bottles accounted for—it was time to hit the rack. Morning comes early on a century.

Getting an early start is one of the keys to a successful ride. You should ride a prescribed route and finish early enough to hit the pool, grab a hearty dinner, hit the hot tub, and then get another good night's rest.

A brief note about equipment: There is one item that is more important than any other. It's not the first aid kit, it's not the tire-patching kit, it's not the extra cushion for your buns— it's not even your bike. It's the "sag wagon," that is, the van (or car pulling a trailer) that accompanies you on the trip. As the name implies, it serves several purposes. One is as a place for tired riders, particularly in hilly country. It can also carry the busted-up bikes when riders crash and burn—or even if they get a simple flat tire. The most important role of the sag wagon, to me anyway, is to carry the previously mentioned snacks and drinks. For the most part, the person driving the wagon is someone who may outwardly make a dramatic show of "giving up" his or her chance to ride the century, but who, in reality, is glad to leave the saddle sores and leg cramps to the others. The driver also gets to start later and arrive first at the lunch stop and, later, at the motel.

Riding this glorious route along the ocean is one tough assignment, eh? Actually, yes. There was a military base for which we needed prior clearance to cross, there were sections of highway where cars and bikes can get a little too cozy, and we encountered several hills that might be a piece of cake to the pros but were actually more like the flip-side of heaven to those of us who are muscularly challenged. I wouldn't recommend more than a neighborhood bike ride for younger kids. Those twelve and older can better handle the traffic and terrain of this type of ride.

If you're looking for a real gut-buster of a ride, try this one on for size. There is a bike ride across the state of Iowa known as RAGBRAI, which stands for Register's Annual Great Bicycle Ride Across Iowa (it's sponsored by the *Des Moines Register* newspaper). The seven-day event is said to be the longest-running, largest (8,500 strong), and oldest bicycle tour in the world. And although it's hard to imagine finding a week's worth of things to do in Iowa, participants make their own fun by making every stop a sort of tailgate party. It's a bit like Mardi Gras—but in a really small town. (And after cycling sixty to seventy miles a day, you won't celebrate quite the same way as you might in New Orleans.) Many people associate Iowa with

Bike Adventure Tips

Here are some tips to keep in mind for long biking adventures:

- When you decide to take a biking adventure, plan it out in as much detail as possible. Check your maps and look for safe spots along the route to take breaks.

- You should never go out with fewer than two riders. This is like the buddy system recommended for swimming safety. Also consider not having too large a group, say more than ten, as this can become a traffic safety problem. The rules of the road apply as much to bike riders as to automobile drivers.

- There's no hard and fast age rule, but I feel around twelve years old is the starting age for the longer, tougher rides. The distance you travel each day is guided strictly by your physical conditioning. (We rode thirty to forty miles each day, finishing early enough to relax around the motel pool and spa.)

- Rear-view mirrors on your bike or helmet are a must, in my opinion. This way, the lead riders will always stay in sight contact with the slower riders. Develop hand signals to alert each other to hazardous road conditions. A single arm pointed toward the pavement alerts those behind you to watch out for glass or other debris.

- The last tip you won't like when the time comes, but do it anyway. After a hard struggle up a steep incline, you'll be hot and sweaty. As you crest the hill and start down the other side, you'll be tempted to open your shirt or jacket and fly down the hill to cool off. Don't. Stay covered. This can chill you and sap your energy for hills yet to come. Plus, you'll look weird.

Happy trails!

sports, cornfields, and flatlands as far as the eye can see. Sports and cornfields, yes; flatlands, no. Some of the hilly regions around the state will take your breath away. One recent event (the route is different each year) began on the western border of Iowa in the town of Sioux City, zig-zagged up and down and across the state, and finished up at the eastern border town of Muscatine. For more information, check out the event's Web site, www.ragbrai.org, which includes lots of information about the ride, the route, and the events, including a link to a virtual tour of each year's route.

Ready for even more adventure on two wheels? For a look at your many options, pick your favorite Internet search site and type in *cycling events across America*. This will lead you to pages and pages of information about events, like an "ultra cycling marathon" that *begins* with a century (see www.ultracycling.com). You'll also find links to info about the bike race across the country that begins in Portland, Oregon, and ends in Gulf Bay, Florida. There's a twenty-four-hour Moab, Utah, event that draws about three thousand participants and probably has more in common with Burning Man—or Woodstock—than it does with an actual bike ride.

In my cycling-related search on the Net, I found an association called Adventure Cycling, a not-for-profit group whose goal is to help you plan a trip wherever you want to go. The organization claims to have a paid membership of around 37,000 people. I have never used this service or spoken with anyone who has, but its Web site is worth a look: www.adv-cycling.org.

Our adventure along the coast highway was all the biking I could handle at the time. The climbs were intense and the feel of the ocean breeze on your face stays with you for a lifetime. So does the feeling of watching your child, the one you taught to ride a bike in the first place, giving you that same self-satisfied smile you saw so long ago. Go for it . . . there's always the sag wagon.

7

Saddle 'Em Up and Move 'Em Out

Tthis chapter is about playing cowboy, er, cowgirl, er, cowperson. Why not head on out to them thar hills to a dude ranch, a friend's ranch, or maybe just to the local pony rides? Kids love to act as though they're a part of the old Wild, Wild West. Luckily for dads, this is an activity where you can participate or just sit back and relax, taking in the sights and smells of the area (well, maybe not the smells) while your kids have a ball. You'll be their hero du jour. (A word of caution here: Make sure that you and your child are ready for the level of horseback riding you choose. This is one of those "do as I say, not as I do" chapters.)

I have a friend who works as a headhunter, but who would really rather be a cowboy (24/7, which his wife would hate—sort of the "Green Acres" syndrome). One winter, he invited my son and me along with him and his own son—the same age as mine—on a genuine cattle roundup at his mountain ranch. Naturally we jumped at the chance. When he asked if we knew how to ride, I scoffed at him, saying, "Of course!" I immediately went out and bought us new jeans and cowboy boots for the adventure.

When we arrived, my friend greeted us with his coterie of cowhands, who proceeded to tell my boy and me that our carefully selected cowboy clothes constituted the absolute worst possible ensemble for the job at hand. They were at least kind enough to spray some water repellant on our boots before we saddled up and headed out.

How many in the audience have seen the movie *City Slickers*? Show of hands, please. Well, that was a walk in the park compared to *this* roundup. These cowpersons made trail boss Jack Palance look like Gwyneth Paltrow in *Emma*.

Our wintry ride began just as it started to rain. There was lots of low, prickly brush growing in the area we had to cover, and the cattle actually hid out *in* the brush. That's where the dogs come in. My friend had about 200,000 dogs—or so it seemed—most of them with some dingo or Australian sheep hound in their bloodline. These dogs were brutal. They hounded the cattle, nipping at their lower legs, driving the cows batty—but, also, out of the brush. One stubborn cow wouldn't budge from the brush, and even tried to attack one of the dogs, cornering it. But just as Bossy was about to stomp the dog, the canine leaped up, clamped down on the cow's lip, and hung on for dear life. The cow went ballistic, wildly swinging its head round and round, up and down (remember Joey Dee and the Starlighters singing "The Peppermint Twist" back in the early sixties?). The dog didn't let go until the cow finally gave up and staggered out of the bushes. Then everyone just started down the mountain like nothing had happened. I was stunned. My son just laughed. I guess I didn't realize I was riding along with a pack of "Doginators."

We rode for a few hours, the rain continued to fall, and the downward mountain trail got slippery. When some of the cattle tried to run away, the more experienced cowboys took out after them. I just tried to stay on my horse. My son was doing just fine—unlike the old block from which he was chipped. We must have ridden for nine hours that day. If you had looked up the word "tired" in the dictionary, my picture would have been missing, covered with the caveat, "Rated R for ragged. This picture is not suitable for viewing by anyone!" In the end, with the aid of the Doginators, we got the cattle down the mountain into a small canyon to contain them for the night.

As they pried me off my horse, I could smell dinner cooking. I hadn't realized we had even reached camp, mainly because it looked more like an abandoned ghost-town building than something living humans would inhabit. But this was the place: broken bed springs covered with torn, thin mattresses, no heat, and rat pellets. Did I mention no heat? My son was having a ball; I just wanted to bawl. I don't remember what we ate, but thankfully I slept like a baby.

The next morning, I was the last one up, and I didn't care. I could hardly move; every bone in my body ached. And once I was up, I could hardly sit. My butt hurt so bad I dreaded getting back on my horse . . . and we had another full day of riding *before* we started on the ride back. Nooooooo!

Horse Sense

If you've never gotten closer to a horse than to admire a pastureful from afar, here's a step-by-step guide to approaching a four-legged friend—and actually hopping into the saddle.

1. **Approach slowly, from the front.** You want the horse to see you coming. (Carrying a peace offering, like a carrot or apple, helps, too.)

2. **Offer the snack to the horse with your hand completely flat.** Horses don't have sharp teeth, but they do love snacks. Keeping your arm extended and your palm flat ensures that you'll go home with all your fingers intact.

3. **Hop on!** Always mount from the horse's left, grab hold of the saddle horn with your left hand, put your left foot in the left stirrup, and lift your body up and over, swinging your right leg over the horse and onto the other side.

4. **Enjoy the ride.** Most trail-experienced horses know exactly where they're going and aren't prone to startling or rearing. The less you worry, and the more relaxed you are, the more fun you'll have.

One thing you should know about me, however, is that when I say I will do something, I give it my all. They would have to shoot me before I'd let anyone else do the work that I had committed to do (although at the time, being shot didn't seem like such a bad alternative). The cowpoke foreman and I had become friends, mostly, I think because he noticed my "non-city-slicker" attitude. He also recognized the walking wounded when he saw me. I nearly kissed that grizzled, stinky old man when he said he needed someone to volunteer to drive the truck back for supplies. (Turns out his smoking, drinking, and carousing years hadn't been kind to him. He was actually two years younger than me.) I waited until the foreman ticked off the reasons he needed everyone else on the ride, leaving only lucky me as the driver. My son had also decided that another day in the saddle didn't sound as fun as it had the previous day, so he became my copilot.

The drive back was no picnic. The route headed the opposite direction of the ranch, over a rocky track that barely resembled a road. But it was better to have my wounded butt on bad truck springs than on a saddle.

After the roundup was completed, we met the guys back at the ranch. My buddy asked if I had enjoyed the adventure. I really had, and told him so. He looked at me kind of quizzically and said, "I thought you told me you could ride?" I looked at him, smiled, checked to make sure my son couldn't hear me, and whispered, "I lied!"

We've been back to the ranch many times since, and each time I've taken one of the kids for the day or the weekend. We even adopted one of the puppies that, according to my friend, wasn't aggressive enough to herd cattle. But that pooch spent his time with us herding and nipping my kids' heels as they walked through the house, so we took him back to the ranch where he became a legendary Doginator among men and cows.

As for taking your kids to a ranch, dude or real, give them riding lessons first, a little at a time. Toughen up your butt pads. You'll be happy you did.

8

Over Easy or Sunny-Side Up?

Here's a weekend activity that everyone will love: cooking. My dad inspired my interest in the culinary arts. Now, Mom was a great cook, but—and I don't know quite how to say this without having every mom in the world hate me for it—as kids, we just *expected* her to be. So, when Dad took over the kitchen, we all sat up and paid attention. If you're a dad who hasn't sliced, diced, or sautéed before, you're in for a treat. No matter what you decide to make, if you're not a regular cook, your kids will be happily amazed that you're in the kitchen at all. You even have my permission, via my Cajun heritage, to burn whatever recipe you attempt and still proudly serve it up as "blackened, Cajun style." Sweet, eh?

Speaking of Cajun food, I have found only one recipe for grits better than mine and that's the one used at the Catahoula restaurant in Napa, California. Catahoula is a breed of dog in Louisiana. If you ever get the chance to see one, watch it

Hit the Kitchen!

Okay, if you're really nice, you can try out this recipe on your kids and tell them that you conjured it up yourself. It looks harder than it really is, but everyone who has tried it has loved it. I prepared it on a television show and it became the show's most requested recipe. Note: Be sure not to mix up the measuring spoons for teaspoons and tablespoons (teaspoons often have the abbreviation *tsp* on the handle; tablespoons have *Tbsp*). Confusing the two could make the difference between eating a delicious meal and tossing away your dinner.

Bob Hilton's Award-Winning Garlic and Ginger-Crusted Salmon

12 garlic cloves, finely chopped
1 cup gingersnap cookie crumbs
2 teaspoons fresh lime juice
2 eggs, beaten
4 salmon fillets, 4 to 8 ounces each
Nonstick cooking spray
13-by-9-inch baking dish
1 cup sour cream
¼ cup mayonnaise
2 teaspoons Caribbean jerk seasoning blend
1 cup chopped mango (fresh or bottled)
1 tablespoon fresh cilantro leaves, chopped

carefully because—I'm serious as a heart attack—it smiles. The owner of the Catahoula restaurant is from the Baton Rouge area of Louisiana and, although this is not a book of endorsements, I heartily recommend his place.

Hit the Kitchen! (continued)

Preheat the oven to 350 degrees. (If you're not too familiar with your oven, keep in mind that you may need to set it on BAKE.) In a small bowl, mix *half* the garlic with the gingersnap crumbs (this is a great chore for one of your kids). Set this aside. In another bowl, whisk the lime juice into the eggs. Dip the salmon fillets into the egg mixture to coat them, then into the gingersnap-garlic mixture, coating both sides.

Spray the baking dish with nonstick cooking spray. Arrange the fillets in a single layer. Bake until the fish is opaque in the center. (You can determine this by piercing the filet with a sharp knife, usually after about fifteen minutes of cooking time). Transfer the fish to a warm serving platter.

While the fish is baking, prepare your sauce. In a small saucepan over medium-low heat, whisk together the remaining garlic, sour cream, mayonnaise, and jerk seasoning until well blended. Stir in the mango and cook until heated through. Spoon the sauce over the fillets and sprinkle the chopped cilantro on top. It looks great and tastes even better.

I have never really cared much for gingersnaps, but in this recipe, they work. As does cooking with your children. Don't be afraid to try this! What is the worst thing that can happen? Have fun; make mistakes. That's why God gave us pizza-delivery people.

I can fry chicken (not as good as my momma's), cook a roast (not nearly as good as my wife's), serve you scallops with roe in a pepper jelly sauce (my own recipe), and more. See the recipe for my award-winning garlic and ginger-crusted salmon with creamy Jamaican mango sauce, pages 38 to 39. It's better than the Catahoula's grits!

But you don't have to get fancy or complicated. The object here is to cook *with your children*. I have my kids help with all the ingredients in my salmon recipe, for example, each for a different part of the preparation. I entered this recipe in a cooking contest in Gilroy, California, the garlic capital of the world, and won the $500 third prize. It actually tasted better than first- and second-place winners. (I know *everyone* says that, but it's true in this case.) By the way, Gilroy is on Highway 101 just south of Los Gatos, which is just south of San Jose, which is just south of San Francisco. The festival takes place in July and is worth attending. The food booths are garlic extravaganzas—they even serve garlic ice cream. I didn't have the guts to try it . . . but I will, one day.

The subject for this chapter occurred to me one evening as I was making garlic toast. (We really do eat some things without garlic, I promise.) I was reheating some spaghetti when I spied some fresh sandwich rolls, and the thought of hot garlic bread slices was too much to resist. I even found some garlic butter in the fridge, and proceeded to toast 'em up. Once the smell of fresh, hot garlic bread wafted through the house, kids started coming out of hiding places I didn't know we had. "Can I have a bite, Dad?" "Can I have half of one, Dad?" "Hey Dad, can I have those last two slices?" Being the nice guy that I am, I said no, and decided, instead, to teach them to fish. Assembly-line style, I showed them how to put some of the hardened butter in a dish and nuke it for a few seconds so that it spreads easily. I taught them how to set the broiler on the stove, how to leave the oven door open just a bit, and, most important of all, how to tell when the toast is *perfectly* done. There is an art, my friend, to broiler toasting, and that will be the subject of my next book, *Broiler Toasting with Bob*. Oprah might want that one also.

If you can spend a bit of time in the kitchen sharing whatever expertise you might have, the rewards are wonderful. I've come home to some "no recipe" cakes that my daughter has literally invented out of her absolutely cute head. And some of them tasted pretty darn good.

One son has taken to spreading his culinary wings by making cheesecakes, candy, and even croissants, which are rather difficult to get just right—and they were. Another son has his dad's old breakfast chef knack. And the other son can warm a mean personal pizza. We have had some wonderful times in the kitchen, including that night with the garlic toast. Don't let your lack of experience stop you. Hit the Web. You can learn how to boil the perfect egg there. Or just make the perfect sandwich together. It's not *what* you do as much as *how* you do it. Make it a huge show as you slather the mayo, Picasso style, across the bread. Then fling open the refrigerator door, grab a slice of individually wrapped cheese of your choice, rip off its cellophane cover, and position it perfectly, much as you would the cornerstone of a cathedral, right on top of a slice of pressed luncheon meat! Do it with panache. Have fun. They will, too.

9

Dr. Strangelove

(Or, How I Learned to Stop Worrying and Love Science Projects)

Some dads beam when their kids are assigned science projects. Unfortunately, I'm not one of them. When I hear the phrase "Dad I've got a science project due next week!" I'm mentally in Hawaii after "I've got." So I've come up with a few "discount" projects that can be fun and make your kids think the old man still has a few tricks up his sleeve.

Let's say you've decided to take a chance and spend a little time in the kitchen after reading the chapter about cooking with your children. You aren't quite brave enough to attempt the salmon recipe, yet, but you have decided to boil up some hot dogs. Gather the kids around to watch the water boil. Once the wieners begin to boogie around inside the pot, "Mr. Science" (that's you) boldly decides to go where this dad has never gone before. Just as you pull the perfectly buttered and toasted hot dog buns from the broiler, condiments at the ready, you look at your children and say, "A penny for my thoughts?" The kids may look at you as if you've finally gone bonkers, but go ahead and ask them, "Okay, then, does any-one have a penny I can borrow?" (Have one ready just in case your kids keep money on them as often as mine do, which is never.) Make sure the penny is an old-looking, dull one, then squirt some ketchup on a paper plate and let the magic begin. Announce that you will now turn this old penny into a shiny new penny, and nonchalantly plop the coin into the ketchup, making sure the penny is totally submerged. Then go about making the hot dogs and consuming them. After this delec-table meal, and their interminable quizzing about how you're going to make the penny experiment work, announce to them that the project is already completed. Tell them to wipe the ketchup off the penny. To their amazement, they'll discover a shiny, brand-new-looking penny. It's a great effect. (And it does make you wonder what all that ketchup might be doing to our stomachs.)

Here's another penny project that's just as amazing . . . and simple. Place ten pennies in a bowl of one-quarter cup vinegar and add a teaspoon of salt. Into the mixture, add a reg-ular old iron nail, and then let the nail and pennies get buddy-buddy overnight. Comes the dawn, the kids will discover that the nail also has a shiny copper coating. You may now explain to them in your most authoritative tone how this works: The vinegar and salt solution dissolves some of the copper molecules from the pennies. And, as we all know, there's nothing more pitiful than lonely molecules with no place to go, so they attach themselves to the nail, and you now have a short penny basket-ball team with one real tall copper center.

Ready to move on, Mr. Science? Here's a great one. The next time you're at the grocery store, buy some juice. It can be any juice that your family likes, but it needs to come in a one-gallon glass bottle, glass being the key to making this project work. Drink the juice and just before putting the bottle in the recycle bin, ask the kids, "Anyone got a boiled egg on them?" They may, but, just to be prepared, have one already boiled and peeled at the ready. To make this project work, the egg must be a little larger than the neck of the bottle. Rip up a little bit of this morning's newspaper—any section but the comics!—and stuff it into the bottle. Using one of those long fireplace-lighting matches, light the paper inside the bottle. Quickly rest the egg on the bottle opening and stand back. What will happen is, the fire sucks out all of the oxygen, creating a vacuum in the bottle, which in turn sucks the larger egg through the smaller opening with a loud sucking sound. You can do this experiment only once per bottle as getting the sooty, blackened egg back out of the bottle isn't a pretty sight.

See, this ain't rocket science . . . but it's fun.

I'll leave you with one more, then you're on your own. If someone in your family uses a hair dryer, borrow it and get either a ping-pong ball or a balloon. This one is so simple, but the kids love it. Turn the hair dryer on, point the air flow upward, holding the dryer waist-high, and then let one of the kids place the ball or balloon over the air flow . . . and let it go. The ball will rise in the heated air stream and continue to hover there. You are now demonstrating what is known in the annals of science as Bernoulli's principle. (Don't you feel smarter already?) Bernoulli was an eighteenth-century Swiss scientist who

Science Fun

There are many activities you can plan with your kids to increase their knowledge of science—and to have fun. Here are just a few ideas:

- Visit a science-related museum together.

- Pick a famous figure in science each month and share that person's contribution with the kids. Get the kids involved by assigning them (or, better yet, letting them choose) one person every couple months or so. Make sure to uncover something fun and unusual about each science person—not just the boring stuff. One thing I recently heard about Einstein, for example, was that he had suits made in exactly the same cut and color, so he wouldn't have to worry about picking out his outfits in the morning. (I'm sure a teen daughter would *love* that!)

- For rainy days when the kids complain there's nothing to do, be sure to have a book with more fun at-home science projects.

- Pick some everyday occurrences, like weather, driving in a car, using a computer, et cetera, and, together with your kids, look up or figure out how they work, scientifically.

- If you live near a scientific laboratory or chemical company, ask about taking a tour. Many are closed to the public, but not all!

discovered that as the velocity of an object increases, the pressure on the other decreases. (Hey, I just read that in the encyclopedia. All I know is the ping-pong ball floats like magic, and the kids like it.)

Be a mad scientist! Wear a smock, spike your hair, have a ball.

10

Experience the Experience!

Spending time with your child doesn't have to mean just the two of you hanging out. In this chapter, we'll talk about how to help your child develop an appreciation of older people—your child's grandparents, older family friends, or seniors you might come in contact with every day in the neighborhood, at the store, or wherever.

Just the other day, my youngest son and I spent some time together loading boxes and some furniture into our van to take them to a storage unit. As we pulled up, the manager, an older gentleman named Tom, came bounding out to greet us. As he welcomed us he was happy to tell us that he was the luckiest man on Earth to have this great job, and to have an apartment, *for free*, above the storage area. Beaming, he added loudly, "I should be paying him (the manager) to let me work here!"

It was a real pleasure to watch as my son listened and talked with Tom. My son clearly appreciated Tom's energy and positive attitude. I imagined it may have helped my son change his view somewhat of senior citizens—and reinforce the fact that they have a lot to teach us "youngsters."

There are lots of ways to help your children appreciate the many stages of aging. Encourage them to get involved with helping seniors in some way. Go with them to visit nursing homes; suggest they volunteer there. Both my mother and my wife's mother are in assisted-living facilities, and even though there are many activities planned daily for the residents, their eyes twinkle most when younger folks come in to talk to them, read to them, or help them with chores. You could even have your children adopt a "grandparent" at a retirement home or in your neighborhood, someone they can visit and check up on occasionally.

It's important that we as parents set good examples for our children when it comes to supporting older people, especially the children's grandparents. For one thing, it gives our children a chance to learn about their own heritage. This gives them a sense of history and helps them understand the sacrifices that those who came before them had to make in order for them to have the lives they have.

What's more, we want them to see how *we* treat *our* parents so our children will treat us with even more respect and understanding. Okay—I know it's a shot in the dark, but it *could* work!

Not all grandparents are always the most delightful people to be around. My wife's mother has always been a bit of a fireball. Each week, we'd have her over for Sunday dinner. The kids rarely stuck around to talk to her after the meal because of her often grouchy mood and her quick, cutting remarks to and about them or us. One such instance happened on one of my son's birthdays. Granny handed him an envelope and told him there was money inside, before he'd even had a chance to open the birthday "surprise." When my son extracted two ten-dollar bills, he smiled and said, "Twenty dollars! Wow, thanks, Granny." Quickly, she yanked one of the bills from his outstretched hand, exclaiming, "I only meant to give you ten. Give me this one back!" And she took the bill and put it in her purse, oblivious to all of our stares.

I wanted to find a way to let my children know that Granny was just being Granny, and that, come what may, we were still a family. So here's the plan I devised. I announced that henceforth, whenever Granny visited, whoever received the worst "Grannyism" of the day would win five bucks (of course, the birthday boy would have won hands down had we been playing that day). Talk about a changed attitude. After that, everyone hung around when Granny visited, actually engaging her in conversation, and later debating how her slings and arrows rewarded them that day. I won the day she said to me, "Mercy, Bob, are you just going to get bigger and bigger?" after I had recently lost ten pounds. My wife won the day she told her mother that a group had offered to fly my wife to another city to be a featured speaker at an event. Without batting an eye, her mother replied, "Well, they'll learn." We did learn to laugh at the situation . . . and make a little money at the same time.

No one likes making sacrifices. But your sacrifice can mean a renewed spirit of survival. Teach your children to value older people—no matter how pleasant or unpleasant they are.

Wisdom of the Ages

If you have elderly relatives, neighbors, coworkers, or acquaintances, you're in luck. Your kid can get a history lesson just by asking these individuals a few questions about their past and the times they've lived through. Here are some good conversation starters:

- How did you feel when you first saw a man walk on the moon?
- What was your first job, and what were you paid?
- What was TV like when it was first available?
- What is a slide rule, a record player, an ice box, a telegram?
- What was school like when you were little?
- What music did you listen to in your teens? What dances did you do?
- How much did a house cost? A car? A movie?

Help them understand the purpose of sacrifice, service, and love. What goes around does indeed come around . . . even in Granny's case. We haven't earned a cent off her in some time now. Maybe she's changed. Or maybe we have. Best five bucks I ever invested.

11

All That Jazz

Rock and roll, country and western, big band, pop, classical, jazz: Music is one of those universal pleasures that's easy to share with your children because they probably already have an appreciation for it in some form. Teach them about music, enjoy music with them, go to a concert, head to the music store together to pick out CDs or tapes.

Where do you start? How about right in your child's room? Depending on the number of children you have, chances are their musical tastes are just as varied. Take my house, for instance. Right at this moment, I could go in to one child's room and hear jazz fusion pounding against walls covered by framed photos of jazz greats. Over in the family room, the CD player is brandishing Britney Spears, sporadically interchanged with Celine Dion and 'N Sync. In the back bedroom, you'll hear the sounds of big band music—one of my loves. And then there's the bedroom at the end of the hall. I'm not quite sure what to make of the otherworldly sounds coming from there.

The point is listening to and talking about music with your children is a natural activity. They probably already like certain music and spend time listening to it. All you have to do is ask them why, what, who—and then ask them to repeat it a few times. Then you've got an activity brewing. You're spending time one on one. That's how you get to know more about them . . . and they get to know more about you.

You can also share an entire weekend of music with your children. Take them to a music performance by an artist or in a genre that you've already studied and listened to together. One of my sons recently surprised me with tickets to a traveling jazz show, featuring music from a CD that he had given me for the holidays. Music is a great thing to share—even if it's *their* favorite, not yours. Our parents didn't understand *our* music, right?

I've always had an appreciation for music. I was a radio DJ for a country music station, a rock and roll station, and even one that played "easy listening" music. (That's also where I used to read the Sunday morning comics on the air. You can read about that embarrassing episode in chapter 26.)

I loved big band music at a time when all of my peers were into Fats Domino and Little Richard. My parents liked county and western music. My brother liked rock. I guess I didn't really turn the corner to rock until I saw Elvis in *King Creole*. I had taken a trip with one of my buddies and his parents to visit relatives in Pearl, Mississippi. He had a girl cousin my age whom I fell "teen-agically" in love with. Her name was Nancy. We all went downtown to see *King Creole* together. She

Helping to Choose Your Child's Instrument

Most music stores will allow your children to hold, fondle, and try the instruments that most interest them. Many will even let you *rent* them, with all the rental fees applied if you decide to purchase the chosen instrument.

When helping your child choose an instrument, keep the following points in mind:

Difficulty level: Although you don't want to quench your child's musical ambition, some instruments might be too difficult for younger children to master and might lead to frustration—and that would defeat the whole purpose.

Size: Make sure the instrument is not too heavy for your child to tote to school, practice, or events—or else you will be the one doing the toting.

One word of caution: Many school band directors try to assign beginning music students to instruments the director *needs* in the band, as opposed to what the child *desires* to play. So start your children on *their* choice of instrument at the beginning of summer, before they join the school band. You may even want to give them private lessons, so they aren't beginners any longer. They are now students of their chosen instrument.

One last tip: Get ear plugs—for yourself. This will help you through the initial years of "Row, Row, Row Your Boat."

loved Elvis, so I learned to love Elvis through her smoldering eyes. Trouble was, she loved Elvis . . . not Bob. Oh well.

In high school, three friends and I joined the SPEBSQSA (Society for Preservation and Encouragement of Barber Shop

Quartet Singing in America). We were good. As a matter of fact, we went to the state high school music competition and rocked 'em good. So good, in fact, that other schools protested our first-place trophy. We did a medley of songs, with choreography yet. If you're into this kind of singing, take one of your children to a barbershop meeting in your local area (for more information, visit www.SPEBSQSA.org). What a great group of people—and what a fun, party bunch. (The ladies' version is known as the Sweet Adeline's.)

I was also in the band in high school and had a ball. We played for all the football games, home and away. I truly enjoyed this experience and have encouraged each of my children to play an instrument in the school band. My wife insisted they take piano lessons, but I wanted them to try band instruments, too. My older son picked the trombone. He and I spent a lot of time together visiting music stores, pricing and trying out different trombones. We finally selected one that we were happy with. He played it for about two months and decided piano was easier.

When my next son was old enough to join the band, he played the trombone we had gotten for Son Number 1, but he didn't really like it. He decided he wanted to play saxophone. So I took him to the same music store to exchange one instrument for the other. He played well . . . for about two years. Then he decided he'd had enough.

Son Number 3 was band age this year, so—you guessed it—saxophone! He wanted to play saxophone. He loved saxophone . . . until a month or so before school started. Then he decided he wanted a trumpet. The music store traded us a brand-new trumpet for his used saxophone. I was thrilled: I had played trumpet in high school. I beamed with the thought that this son was following in his old man's footsteps. Once school began, he decided music just didn't fit into his class schedule. (He is making straight A's, but I still wish he'd found time for band.)

Just before Christmas this year, I asked him if he was ever going to play trumpet in the band. He beat around the bush for a while before finally admitting that he really didn't want to. I asked him again, just to make sure. Again, he said no, and asked why I was smiling. I told him, "No particular reason," which wasn't true at all.

I shared my plan with my wife, got her approval, and took the trumpet that had been a saxophone that had been a trombone . . . and traded it for a beautiful, brand-new guitar—for myself. My wife then "gave" it to me for Christmas. I haven't learned to play a single note on it yet, but *one* of these days, I'll learn a few chords. I might even break out with a little "If you're lookin' for trouble" from *King Creole*. I even know how to curl my lip. Eat your heart out, Nancy.

12

Changes

You may find it difficult to make this jump with me, but the point of this chapter is to spend a weekend with your children . . . teaching tolerance. We need tolerance in all stages of our lives: at school, at work, and at home. Hey, there are even museums dedicated to this concept. Imagine how difficult it must be for people who are ostracized because they look, feel, or act differently than the masses do. Taking your children to libraries, exhibits, or movies that teach this valuable concept is rewarding for you personally and as a dad. You'll instill tolerance in your children, who will hopefully do the same with their children.

Now I don't mean to discount the importance of teaching tolerance by tying it to what may seem an insignificant issue to everyone else. It certainly wasn't insignificant to my family.

In the chapter about music, when I mentioned the sounds of Britney Spears and 'N Sync, you probably guessed that those were my daughter's musical choices. At that writing, that's what she liked. Since then, she's undergone a dramatic change in musical taste. Now, rather than Spears and Sync (sounds like the making of another group!), it's the Dixie Chicks and Garth Brooks. My little girl has discovered country music.

As trivial as it may sound to you, this has become a major disruption in our family. As I mentioned before, I was, for a short while, a country music DJ. It happened by accident. I had worked for a radio station before joining the Navy and was offered my old job back when I got out. By then, though, the station had completely changed its format. Now, rather than Mathis and Miller, it was Waylon, Willie, and the Boys. I took the job, with reservations, and much to my surprise, began to like the sound.

Fast forward to being married to my Eternal Sweetie. She loves Pavarotti and Previn and blanched at the sound of Paycheck and Parton. But as a birthday surprise to me one year (a true understatement here), she spent weeks and weeks writing songs and rehearsing with a motley group of musicians preparing to show what a great sport she was by . . . well, you might not believe what she did. She had three couples pick us up one evening and we all drove to this dumpy, dirty, dank nightclub (another understatement). At one point the band announced that they were going to take a break, and my wife slipped off to the ladies' room. As the band started up again, much to my surprise, the lead "guitarist" announced, "Ladies and gentlemen, we here at the (I won't give the name of the club, to protect my family from potential lawsuits) are proud to introduce America's newest sangin' star, Starla Shane!" And through the curtain and the band's cigarette smoke, nervously approaching the microphone, was my beautiful bride wearing a black western dress, black hat, and black pointy-toed suede cowperson boots. What a hoot! She was terrific. (We've got a video of her performance that night. Whoever buys the most copies of this book wins a private screening of the part where she sings "Pay Day." It's actually purty dang good!)

The point of this story is to demonstrate how unusual it was for a member of our family to love this country music. And now, it's baaaaaack. My three sons cannot believe the twangy sounds that emanate from my little princess's room. The boys roll their eyes and try to avoid passing her room, which is rather tough considering that their bathroom is down the hall from it. This is where teaching tolerance comes in: one-on-one time spent with each boy pointing out how his choices, while great for him, could be interpreted as dubious by others. I want them to understand how the baby of the family, standing tall against the choices of her siblings, must be able to make those choices for herself, without pressure from the rest of us to do things differently.

For my daughter, it was one of those times when, as Otis Redding said, "You got-ta, got-ta, got-ta, try a little tenderness." She was feeling ostracized, so I took her out for a day trip. We drove around, shopped a little, grabbed some snacks—but mostly we listened to country music. I reassured her that her choices were valid, so long as they were chosen for the right reasons. We also decided to open an after-school cookie and lemonade stand on the corner of our lot, hoping to make

Teaching Tolerance

Too few parents today are teaching tolerance to their kids, or the all-important compassion we need for those who are different. When your children come across someone disabled, deformed, mentally challenged, or in any way unusual, teach them the following:

- Never stare or point at anyone.
- Always smile and be friendly; you'll be amazed at the returns.
- Never join in teasing, and silence others who do.
- Remind your kids that outside appearances are not as important as inner qualities, and that inside we're all the same.

enough money to go to the upcoming Garth Brooks concert together.

This D-I-V-O-R-C-E (can't you just hear Tammy Wynette sangin' that?) between our daughter and smutty pop music is actually pretty cool. I can't count the times when I'd turn the car radio off to avoid listening to some of the childish babble going out over the airwaves. These DJs apparently couldn't care less that kids tuning in to their often sexually titillating comments littered with foul language emulate them in their actions, reactions, and language at school and elsewhere.

My daughter now says she wants to be a country singer when she grows up. When I wrote the other music chapter, she had wanted to be Celine Dion. I'm sure she'll change her mind again, at least once or twice.

So where did this weekend of teaching tolerance take us? My sons still look at my daughter like she's from Pluto when she plays her music, but she's okay with that. As for her mom and me, soon as I figure out two more chords on my geetar, me, Starla, and little Starlette are headin' over to audition for the Grand Ol' Opry.

13

Ladies and Gentlemen, on Your Right...

That's right, take your children on a tour. Every city has some kind of something to tour. In our town, we have the railroad museum and the Old Town area with historic buildings, fish hatcheries, and much more. Not too far from us is the site where gold was discovered in California, and a bit farther up the road from there is the site where the Donner party made the dark side of history trying to get through a snowstorm in covered wagons. Just a hop, skip, and a jump—mostly a jump—away, is the site of the annual frog-jumping contest in Calavaras County. Toward the Bay Area sits Petaluma, infamous for its arm-wrestling championships.

So what do you have where you live? Think about it. Call your tourism bureau, your chamber of commerce, city hall, even your police department. I bet you'll be surprised to find that there is a lot more to do in your area than you might have suspected.

I once met a man as our family was touring New York City. We had taken the ferry to see the Statue of Liberty. He and I were both standing near the base of the statue, looking up, and I said how impressive this monument was to me. He agreed and told me he had lived in New York City for many years, moved away, and now was back as a visitor, seeing the statue up close and personal for the very first time. Amazing!

A few years back, when we lived in a small town in Iowa, I called the local nature center. We had bats in our hundred-year-old house. They lived in the space between the walls and we could hear them scratching inside the walls at night. Sometimes, they would burst out into flight while we were sleeping, swooping across our bedroom with a scary rustling of wings. Depending on which room the bats invaded, you'd hear varying tones of petrified shrieks from little boy to bigger boy, from little girl to big mama, and then everyone would come tumbling into our bedroom to duck under our covers, leaving me to fend off the vampires. A friend told me the best way to get rid of bats was to work on my tennis serve and backhand (wink, wink). I will not tell you whether I tried this method. Let's just say that I had to repair quite a large ding in our beautiful antique dresser.

The bats in our belfry were the reason I decided to take my kids on a tour of the nature center. The center just happened to be having a slide show about bats. I thought this would be a good chance to see the little buggers up close and personal, to see how cute bats are, so none of us—uh, I mean *them*—would be afraid again. Have you ever seen a close-up of a bat's mouth—fangs, saliva, and all? Needless to say, we *all* left there more frightened than when we arrived. (I didn't say all of the time you spend with your children would have a positive outcome, did I?)

But I've taken my kids on lots of tours. We've seen the Jelly Belly factory (and left with the Jelly Belly ache) and the Liberty Bell in Philadelphia (someday, I'll tell you the story of my sons nearly giving the Liberty Bell guard a heart attack as they crossed under the protective rope on a mission to ring out the sounds of freedom throughout the land). We've even been through the Hershey chocolate factory in Hershey, Pennsylvania. That had to be one of the most anticipated tours we've ever gone on. The closer we got, the more excited we became. Imagine, more chocolate than you could ever eat! Impossible! As we were just a few miles from the factory, I told the kids, "Let's roll down our windows and see who smells chocolate first!" Now, stop and think for a moment. Besides chocolate, what is one of the main ingredients in milk chocolate? Milk, of course! Where does milk come from? Cows! And what do cows do a lot of after eating a lot of hay? Right! And that's what we smelled, until we wised up and closed the windows, which didn't take us long.

I remember my dad taking me to visit his brother at Louisiana State University one summer. Uncle Berry was a professor at the ag extension program where he worked on different types of animal/food experiments. I was speechless when he showed me a three-legged chicken. (I never did find out if the Colonel was funding that particular research.) My most vivid memory is of Uncle Berry stepping into a huge cooler that had droplets of water rolling down the outside of its metal door from the heat and humidity of the Louisiana summer. As he stepped back out, the cold air from inside the cooler collided

Be a Tourist in Your Own Town

I guarantee there are hundreds of tours you can take your children on, no matter where you live. Fun tours are out there; you just have to be creative. Here are some interesting locations you may not have considered:

- Auto wrecking yard
- Butcher shop
- Bakery
- Dairy or produce farm
- Factory of any kind
- Plant nursery
- Police/fire department
- Airplane hangars
- Candy makers
- Animal breeders
- Computer chip manufacturers
- Post office
- Race track
- Newspaper
- Fish hatchery

with the hot air outside, creating what looked like a small storm cloud. Uncle Berry emerged like a vision through the cloud with both of his hands stretched out before him. In each hand was an icy glass bottle, about 12 ounces I would guess, containing the richest, sweetest, most deliciously cold chocolate milk I had—and have—ever tasted. Dad and I gulped down that sweet elixir, and when Uncle Berry told us we could have as much as we wanted, we helped ourselves to some more. It was great fun being with my dad that day.

Driving home from San Francisco recently with my wife, we crested a hill and saw a sign for a dairy. I immediately thought of the visit to Uncle Berry and the cold, delicious chocolate milk. I had a sudden urge to stop and sample the dairy's chocolate milk, but I decided to wait and take my kids there another time. Who knows? Maybe that will be their tour of a lifetime.

Sometimes tours can take you by surprise. One day, my wife awoke with a nasty cold, so I jumped into action to take over as one of the drivers for my daughter's school field trip. Driving three giggling, yelling, and teasing nine-year-old girls around had not been on my agenda for the day—or *any* day as a matter of fact. As we drove toward Sacramento's historic Old Town, I thought I'd try something and began to talk to the girls about opera. They knew very little about it, so I asked if I could play them a selection or two. One of my very favorite CDs is *The Ultimate Divas Album*. I selected my absolute favorite selection on the disc, Sumi Jo singing from Mozart's "Die Zauberflote" ("The Magic Flute") in the *Queen of the Nights Revenge Aria*. I talked to the girls about musical instruments, the flute in particular, and explained that that is the sound the singer makes with her voice. I was surprised by how quiet and attentive the girls became as the song began. Utterly inspiring music and such clarity of voice. Even if you hate opera, this selection could make you love it—well, at least like it. The girls did, a lot. We talked about what they had just heard, and we listened to a few more selections before we reached our destination.

The field trip took place at the Discovery Museum; the tour focused on the discovery of gold in California. In addition to all of the gold paraphernalia on display, one of Eric Heiden's *five* Olympic gold medals, plus his antiquated-looking racing skates, also were afforded a spot. Heiden was a three-time world speed skating champion as well as the 1980 Olympic hero, and he is now an orthopedic surgeon in our city.

Surprisingly, on the ride back, my daughter sat up front with me and we talked and held hands while her two friends giggled and teased each other in the back seat. My daughter told me how she had beamed with pride when the docent mentioned the Armour meat packing company in her talk about businesses during the gold rush. She beamed because she knew her granddad, my father, had worked for that company all of his career. I beamed, proud of her.

The trip to the Discovery Museum was an unplanned tour, but a wonderfully enjoyable one. If you still don't have an idea of what might make an interesting tour for you and your kids, check your local yellow pages (and see "Be a Tourist in Your Own Town," on page 63)—there are a million ideas. After that, all you have to do is yell, "Hey kids, road trip!" and let the fun begin.

14

I'm Sorry, Please Forgive Me

The weekend comes and you've been looking forward to relaxing, catching up on chores, or just gorking out and doing absolutely nothing. That's *your* plan. But, unbeknownst to you, this is *not* your children's plan.

You walk in the door and it's WWIII . . . or at least, the WWF! It's "Dad" this and "Dad" that, do this, come here, go there—relaxing weekend plans, my patootie! All you wanted to do was catch your breath for perhaps two, maybe three seconds, but noooooo! The rug rats have seen the enemy and it is you. *Attack!!!*

Does this sound familiar? How can you even attempt to plan an activity with your children when you feel ganged up on from the minute you come home? Your temper immediately starts to escalate, your mood darkens, perhaps your tongue becomes a bit too sharp for your family's good. Hold on a second, bucky-boy. It's time to drop back ten yards, set the laces on the ball, and punt.

Step out of yourself for a moment and be a ghost hovering over this scene. Actually, start hovering about a half-hour before you arrive home. What you'll probably see is your kids gleefully anticipating your arrival: "Daddy's coming home soon!"

Watch as you drive up. The buzz begins as the car door slams. The key slides into the lock as in slow motion. As the teeth of the key make soft, scraping sounds against the brass of the lock, heads whip around in that sound's direction, eyes wide, brows heightened, hair flying out from their heads as they redirect their momentum toward the front door. Tennis shoes squeak as children pirouette anxiously, waiting for the curtain to rise and the star of this family ballet to make his entrance. His lines are anticipated as being . . .

"Behold my clan, I, your great and powerful leader, have come home with meat and treasures." He smiles, lifting and kissing each child, laughing and tossing them roofward, catching them in his big, powerful, loving hands.

Cut! Print! That's a wrap!

Actually, let's do a second take on how that scene is actually played out.

Everything is the same . . . until the door swings open. They run toward you, yelling and screaming who knows what all—and you come unglued.

"Can't I walk in the *$@#*% door without being run over?! Give me some time to catch my breath!! *Back off!!!*"

All right, take a deep breath. Now, take a look and see what's really going on here. You've had the entire day away from home to "catch your breath." It's time to get your priorities straight.

1. Family first.

2. Everything else, second.

Now that we have that straight, let's spend some time, one on one, mending the little hearts that you've just broken. Their hero has just returned—and chewed them out for being excited about his return. That doesn't make a lot of sense, now does it?

It's hard to admit that you're wrong, but if situations like this ever arise in your home, you are. But what a great opportunity you now have. Apologize to your children, en masse, and again individually. Say these exact words:

"I'm sorry. I love you. Please forgive me."

Tell each child again how much you love him or her, adore that child, and relish spending time with him or her. Teach your children that even parents can make mistakes, that we can be wrong sometimes. Talk about your job and career with them, and explain the stresses of your day. Just don't let them think you're trying to *justify* coming home as a grouch. Let this be an opportunity to take them on a drive, a walk, a bike ride, whatever—anything that will reassure them that *they* are indeed the most important thing in your life.

In doing this, you'll accomplish many things. For instance, you will now absolutely have a changed outlook on coming home from work. You may love your job, but now you'll realize that you're coming home to your "real" job, as a daddy. You might learn to "air out" your work frustrations on the drive home, enabling you to walk through the door with the smile they are hoping to see. And you'll mean it. You will reinvigorate your children's love and admiration for you, and

What to Do When You Screw Up

I'm not suggesting you go out and buy each child an expensive present or immediately take them down to the ice cream parlor every time you snap at them or make a mistake. (In fact you probably don't want to set *that* pattern . . . those crafty kids might start looking *forward* to the times when Dad goes ballistic!) There are lots of ways you can show that you're sorry and reinforce your love when you've acted harshly or blown up unprovoked. Here are a few ideas to get you started:

First, apologize. I said this already, but this is the most important part. Don't wait to do this!

Talk to each child individually. Shortly afterward, make time to talk to each child involved in your blowup separately. Visit their rooms, suggest a short walk around the block—whatever you have to do to get them alone. Allay their fears that you may still be angry. Ask their forgiveness. Tell them you love them.

Have a sense of humor about it. If you can laugh about the incident with your children later, that sends the message that it was *not* serious, that you *didn't* mean it, and that it's just one of those embarrassing emotional outbursts that happen in every family once in a while.

Make a habit of saying "I love you." This means *not* just when you're asking for forgiveness. How often you tell them you love them will depend on your personality, of course, but it's a good idea to get used to saying it. Kids love to hear it, and, contrary to what you might think, it does *not* lose its meaning the more you say it!

yours for them. But, most important, you'll set an example for how the rest of your family's generations will be treated by their dads. It's the old "give a fish/teach to fish" scenario . . . and you're the fishing boat captain.

Okay, the hook's baited. Smile and relax. All you have to do now is let your line out, set the hook, and your catch is guaranteed to be bountiful.

15

The Christmas Rat

Holidays are a great time to plan activities with your children. On the Fourth of July, I make sure to take the kids to whatever patriotic event might be going on in our community. For the past few years we've congregated with neighbors at our area park for a day of patriotism, picnics, and games. Last year, I participated with other dads, as well as our children, in a reenactment of the signing of the Declaration of Independence. It was really effective—and an easy and fun way to teach our kids some history. Here's how I did it:

I lined up a number of children and dads equal to the number of signers of that precious document. As I read to the assembled throng how this event came to be, I included what happened to these men who so courageously put their lives, as well as their names, on the line. Because of their involvement, most of them suffered losses—of family, property, or even their own lives—so that we might have a guaranteed future of freedom in this land. And then I read off each signer's name as those lined up to represent them verbally responded with an enthusiastic "aye" or "yes," punctuating their affirmation of our declared independence. It was quite a thrilling experience! I watched as both parents and children, beaming with pride, gave voice to those honorable men who had the will to choose to do what was right more than 200 years ago. It was indeed a liberating day for my children and me, truly a weekend to remember.

Every holiday can present a variety of ways to make it extraordinary for you and your children. One such way for us began with a tradition between my children and my wife. Ever since the oldest was the youngest, my wife has gleefully gotten out the watercolor paints the day after Thanksgiving and—first with the first child, then adding in numbers two, three, and four as they came of age—painted holiday scenes on our front windows. These scenes included Christmas trees decked with ornaments, presents, bells—anything "holidayish." That is, until the rat came along.

Now the rat isn't really a rat. It is, or rather was intended to be, a mouse: the Christmas mouse. However, one Christmas six or seven years ago, the mouse came out looking a little more like a rat, to everyone's amusement. (Well, my wife was a little less amused than the rest of us; after all, she painted the rat, er, mouse.) The next year, the kids began begging for the Christmas rat again, and even though my wife did her best to make it look like a mouse, it was forever more, officially, a rat. Now my wife even calls it a rat (which takes some of the fun out of it for the kids, of course).

My role in the tradition came about through my assigned part of the job. As my wife is the artist (please use the French pronunciation: ar-TEEST), I am the "WY-purr" of the rat. In other words, I wipe up the mess she and the kids make! I tried to figure out how to make the cleanup job as fun as the paint job, and finally hit on it last year.

Now, each year after Thanksgiving, it's time to "paint the Christmas rat." On January 1, New Years Day, it's time to "kill the rat." I buy scrapers for the children and me, and we attack the painting, furiously scraping the painted scene off the windows until they're clean. Everything but the rat. In the end, all that remains is the rat, floating in a sea of windows.

I then hold out a paper bag, letting the kids draw numbers, so that we may attack the rat piece by piece in an orderly way. A leg here, a tail there, one ear then the other, then an eye. The tip of the nose is a favored piece for some reason, but the coup de rat, of course, as the kids scream with laughter, is . . . the rat's hind end. Don't ask me why, it's just a brown painted blob as far as I'm concerned. But as each kid takes his or her turn, and they get closer and closer to being the one who gets to scrape off the "you-know-what," they get amazingly creative in their attempts to save enough paint to put them into the gold medal position. This year, the oldest boy kept saying how stupid this whole thing was—all the while anxiously waiting his turn to see if he'd get the RB (rat's butt).

It's not much, but it *is* an hour of silly fun together. My daughter protests the entire time, claiming it's cruel to the poor rat, yet, there she is, smile on face, scraper in hand, waiting her turn along with the rest of us.

Isn't it great that we dads can get away with such antics? Weekends can be fun without a whole lot of effort. Just mix in

Start Your Own Holiday Tradition

One of the best ways to establish a family tradition is to do something with your kids that your parents did with you: Christmas caroling at a retirement home, hiding a special Golden Egg among the regular hard-boiled ones at Easter, or designating each child to be the ambassador of a certain holiday and letting him or her dream up a new "tradition." (Hint: These traditions don't even have to coincide with national holidays. Make your own!) Here are a few more ideas:

New Year's giveaway. Instead of making New Year's resolutions you know you'll break (Have you lost those ten pounds yet?), resolve to select at least one toy, book, piece of sports equipment, or other item that gathers dust around the house and give it away. Before you make the donation, schedule a family show-and-tell time where everyone explains the reason for choosing the item and what he or she hopes another child or family will get out of it.

Spring fling. It's the first day of spring. Depending on where you live, you'll either feel it or you won't (especially if you live in the Midwest). You and your kids can celebrate anyway—regardless of whether the trees are starting to bloom and the birds are beginning to sing. This can be as silly as gathering everyone together and literally flinging yourselves (one by one!) onto the couch, or a bit more organized, like having a family party and decorating with paper flowers, birds, and butterflies.

Halloween scream. This may not be the smartest tradition to start when your kids are little enough that they still scare easily. But once they've toughened up a bit, you can make it a family affair to scare the pants off the rest of the kids in the neighborhood on October 31. Each year, devise a scary scene at the entrance to your home for trick-or-treaters. You could even put on a haunted house.

a little mischief with a lot of love and care, and you'll be amazed at what pops up. I know that because of my wife's and my silliness, my kids will keep the tradition of the Christmas rat going in their own families. I already know that one of my gifts to my yet-unborn grandchildren will be window scrapers.

16

R.E.S.P.E.C.T.

Aretha Franklin had it right. Respect is what it's all about sometimes. Sock it to me, sock it to me, sock it to me! (If you haven't heard the song, you'll have no idea what that's all about. If you haven't heard the song, shame on you!) This weekend idea involves several elements, and it's intended primarily for sons, but it'll work, in a roundabout way, for daughters also. I'm talking about teaching your sons to respect women (and to show it!), to their mothers in particular. Your goal is to teach them to value *all* women. This will help them when they start dating, get engaged, get married, and have a family of their own. Your daughters will benefit from your lessons by realizing their own worth and knowing that they deserve to be treated well by their dates or mates.

I long ago realized that to win an argument was actually to lose it. In a relationship, when someone wins, it's always at the other person's expense. So I have determined that—buckle those seat belts for this one, guys—my wife is *always right!*

There, I've said it. This is not being deceitful; it's being smart. This precludes your children growing up in a hostile environment as their parents brood and grumble for days over piddling little disagreements that, over time and without resolution, become as explosive as Mount Vesuvius. More often than not, as I defer to my wife, she in turn defers to me, and rather than an explosive situation, love is in the air in our home. And respect.

Show your children how you value your mate. Let them see that the two of you are a team. This does two things. One, it gives the children a feeling of confidence and security. Two, it lets them know that "Mommy said it was okay with her if it's okay with you," and vice versa, won't cut it in this house. United we stand. Let the children see you open the door for your sweetheart, teach them why you walk on the street side of the sidewalk while she walks on the building side. Stand when she enters the room, help her with her chair and her sweater or coat. Do everything you can to make her feel cherished and adored, and make sure your children are aware of it each and every time. Teach the boys to do the same for their mom, and they can even try some of their newfound gentlemanliness on their sister. Respect breeds respect.

And then, the ultimate test. Tell the boys that today is Mom's day off and that they are going to learn what it takes to be the CEO of this major corporation called Home. You are now going to teach the boys how to be men. You are going to teach them the secrets of . . . how to clean a house. (I learned this early on and actually knew more about it than my wife when we married. It was a real thrill to overhear my sweetie thanking my mom for rearing a man who knew how to make a home sparkle.) So here we go.

Okay, I'll pause a moment while your heartbeat goes back to normal. Your question to me just might be, How can you teach what you don't know? Don't worry, be happy! First, get on the Web and hit your favorite search engine. I typed in phrases like *how to do laundry, how to mop, how to make a bed,* and so on, and each time got tons of information back. If you want to skip all of that "difficult" research, call the bookstore and ask for *Housekeeping Secrets My Mother Never Taught Me* (Prima Publishing, 2001). I wholeheartedly endorse this book because 1) it actually shows you how to do every chore in the house, 2) my wife wrote it, and 3) I gave her much of the information for all the how-to's. You too can become an expert using either system, but learn before you try to teach. Now— here we really go!

Housekeeping 101: If you turn it on, turn it off. If you drop it, pick it up. If you dirty a dish, wash it. Basically, don't wait for someone else to do your job. Pick up after yourself as you go. I've always asked my kids: How can you find time to do a job the second time if you can't seem to find time to do it right the first time around? Respect!

The first stop: Familiarize your children with household cleaning products. You simply *must* go over each and every product, what it does, and the hazards of same if you want the job done right.

Next, show them how to use the broom, the vacuum, and the mop. I got my kids' attention by showing them how, as a Navy swabbie, I learned to splay out the mop, spinning it with

Little Helpers

On days when you just want your kids to clean their rooms, here are the top five ways, guaranteed to reveal that they actually have carpet in their rooms.

1. Announce that anything left on the floor will be donated to charity the next day.

2. Scoop up their stray belongings and sell them back to the kids for a dollar each, thereby helping to fund their own allowance.

3. Provide plenty of labels, bins, and boxes to help them get organized.

4. Set a timer and offer a reward if the room is cleaned within a set time.

5. Keep a donation bag handy for filling with outgrown toys and clothes.

a great flourish, leaving the mop head swirled out on the floor and the handle dangling free in space. The problem with this approach, of course, is that they then spent too much time working on the splaying rather than the swabbing.

Teach them how to clean the toilet bowls, lid up and lid down. This might give them an appreciation of why women care so much about lid positions. Do your children know how to make a bed? No, I mean *really* make a bed? Teach them how to take the top sheet, tuck in under at the end of the bed, and then put the "touch of the master bed maker" on it. There should be seven to ten inches of sheet hanging over each side of the bed. On each side, lift the sheet about one foot from the end of the bed, and tuck the part of the sheet left dangling under the mattress. This will help keep the sheet firmly tucked under the mattress and gives the bed a crisp look.

Sweeping, mopping, dusting—it all takes time, but needs to be done. Do your kids do their own laundry? This is an important lesson, followed by how to iron their own clothes. My kids all press their own shirts for church. Partly it's because they know how, but mostly they do it because I've told them that if they don't have the inclination to hang up their clothes, I don't have the inclination to pay for the cleaners. Works!

There are several things going on during this "boot camp"-style weekend. First, they'll understand firsthand how much work Mom does. They need to know that the wonderful meal they just devoured in seconds flat represented several hours of time and energy on someone's—usually Mom's—part. They need to know how much you love and respect their mom, your love and best friend. They need to know how to value their most precious asset—today their mom, tomorrow their mate—and help build their own lifelong partnership by sharing in the effort of running a home.

Spend a weekend teaching them R.E.S.P.E.C.T. and you'll reap a lifetime of rewards, for them and for you.

Now here's the best part: Mom comes back home at the end of her day off and stands agog, checking out her sparkling home. She smiles at you, gives you that knowing wink, thanks the children profusely, and the two of you sneak away to the back of the house. Once inside, you lock the doors, kick off your shoes, turn on the stereo, and begin to slide in stocking feet across freshly swept, mopped, and waxed floors, to the thump-thump-thump of Aretha. Yeah! *Sock it to me, sock it to me, sock it to me!* (Look, you've *got* to buy the CD or call the oldies station.)

17

Survival of the Fittest (Yes, I Mean You!)

Two very different books motivated me to write this chapter. One was a Christmas gift, the other was a loaner. The loaner book, *Return with Honor*, told the saga of Air Force Captain Scott O'Grady. You might remember his story from the news a few years back: His F-16, one of America's premier fighting aircraft, was shot down over Bosnia. After surviving a rocket blast through the "belly of his fuselage," ejecting at a "slowed-down" speed of around 350 miles per hour, and landing amid armed men, he survived for six harrowing days and nights. Had he not had the superb survival training gained in his years in the military, and his incredible faith, he might not have lived to tell his tale. Read this book. Read this book to your children. They will learn about a true American hero.

The other book, the Christmas gift, was actually meant to be a joke (I hope). It's titled *Survival*, and it's a how-to field manual from the Department of the Army. Reading either book is rather chilling, when you think that people have actually done these things to stay alive. After watching that CBS show *Survivor*, then reading these books, you realize how trivial television makes the true art of survival. This is one very good reason to base a weekend with your kids on learning survival skills.

I hope and pray that we as a nation, or we as a collective family, never have to go to the extremes that our fighting forces are trained to encounter. We must always be prepared spiritually, financially, emotionally, and have enough food, water, and first aid supplies to protect us in the event of some future act of terrorism or calamity; for ourselves as well as our neighbors.

With that in mind, how about putting your kids through a "survivor camp" to teach them a few of the more important things they can use in an emergency situation? For this weekend activity, don't worry about the weather forecast. Just factor the weather in as one of the survival lessons:

Heat: Deal with severe sunburn, heat exhaustion, or dehydration (see item on water that follows).

Rain: Deal with soggy clothes, wet bedding, and cooking in the rain.

Snow: Stay warm in freezing weather (and avoid frostbite!).

Knowing how to get around safely during hazardous weather conditions is a must, whether hiking, cycling, or just taking a walk around the block.

If you choose an unfamiliar location for your weekend of training, the first question to ask your children on arrival is:

Where are we? Ask them if they can remember any of the landmarks you passed on the way in. Have them identify roads or types of landscapes, anything that might give searchers a clue if they were lost but able to make a cell phone call or use walkie-talkies to call for help.

Some of the quick lessons to teach them include navigation, finding water, finding food, making a fire, and improvising shelter. I'll provide some information here, but you can check most any Boy Scout store outlet (they're in your phone book or on the Web). They have tons of information about these items. You can hit the Web or visit camping and sporting goods stores to find all the survival gear you'll need. (Also see "A Survivalist's Checklist," page 85.)

Don't frighten your children while you impart this information. As a matter of fact, teaching them to be calm and clear-minded in stressful situations gives them much better chances of survival.

Here are a few things you might include in the lesson plan during your survivalist weekend:

Navigation. First things first. Stop, sit, think. Remember your first question? Where are we? Think about everything you've seen and passed. Survey the area. Climb to the highest point you can safely get to and look around. Safety is of utmost importance. A fall, a cut, a broken bone—these accidents change the odds for a quick and safe rescue. If you were smart enough to bring along a map, take that with you to the high point and see if you can turn the map so that it fits into the landscape that

A Survivalist's Checklist

If you're planning to take one or more children on a survivalist weekend, here's a list of essentials. (Remember, you don't want to make the weekend too scary—I'm not suggesting you take your children to the woods, dump them off, and say, "See if you can get home, kids!")

- Area map
- Compass
- Water (in a reusable container, like a canteen)
- Sharp knife
- Shovel
- Tent or tarp
- Matches
- Comfortable hiking shoes
- Extra socks (wool or specially engineered polyester, like Cool Max, is best)
- Hooded parka or water-resistant jacket
- Camera or camcorder to record all the fun

you're looking across right now. It's best if you teach by having them do all of the hands-on work. Buy a compass and bring it with you. Show them how to adjust the map, lining up the map's compass (look in the lower corner of the map) with your physical compass. This will give you the true heading of where you are and where you want to be. There's not enough space to elaborate fully here, so pick up the brochure that came with your compass and study it carefully.

Teach the kids how to navigate by the stars. This will necessitate more than just a daytime survival lesson, obviously, but what a treat it will be for them and for you. One of my favorite scenes from a recent movie is from *A Beautiful Mind*. This particular scene has the main character standing outside at night with his arm around his soon-to-be wife, looking at the stars. He tells her to look at the night sky and say any shape—an umbrella, a dog, a flower. When she does, he takes her hand in his, points to the stars, and, like an artist painting with their clasped fingers, immediately connects her mind's eye to the object of her desire.

Pointing out the major constellations will be thrilling to youngsters who aren't familiar with them. And you'll have a right to be impressed with yourself, too.

Water. Without water, you die. Drink the wrong water, you die. Teach your children about safe drinking water, safe plants, and roots that may contain a source of liquid, and where to dig or how to catch water. Concentrate on the topography and plant life of your particular area.

Food. This might be a great way to get your kids to visit a nature center with you without them realizing they are studying nature. If they think it's only for the survival course, so much the better. Wild plants, flowers, berries, and nuts are in abundance in most areas. They might not like salads at home, but pulling up a wild tuber and wolf-ing it down—now that's cool.

There are a million other ideas that you can try. Whether or not you're an outdoorsy dad, your survivor camp can build some great memories . . . and perhaps even save a precious life one day. Remember, treat this as a fun excursion and don't get upset if they don't take it as seriously as you might want them to. Just make sure they learn the basics and have a good time doing it. If they enjoy it, they will ask for more. More lessons, more time with you—and less time vegging out in front of the idiot box watching a bunch of adults gripe and moan about being hungry and dirty, showing your kids that they don't have a clue about how to really survive.

Rather than voting people off the island, you're teaching your kids that sticking together is what it's really all about. Now *that's* survival.

18

Please Do Feed the Animals

My daughter Nicole loves animals, absolutely adores them. She's only nine years old, but she's already talking about "when she moves out." This is so that she can build a gigantic house, which at this point stands to be about ten thousand square feet, four stories tall, with individual rooms for each of the many animals she plans to own. She has also decided to buy an old school bus so that she can transport all of her animals with her wherever she might roam. On and on this fantasy goes and where it stops nobody knows.

Sweet and cute, right? What's the problem here, you ask? The problem is that, as it is with 99 percent of all children her age, *they don't take care of the animals they already have. We have to!* (As I write this, I'm listening to the sweet "who-eeee" sounds of my wife as she slogs through the mess that is our little beast-master's guinea pig cage.)

Okay, okay, I know, our parents probably had to do the same thing for us, but how can we break this pet-trified cycle?

Take 'em on a weekend excursion to the ASPCA. My wife's initial reaction to this idea was, "This will only make her want *more* animals!" (At the time we already had one dog, two Russian tortoises, three-and-a-half cats (one now lives at the neighbor's house because it hates the dog), and Woody, the guinea pig. My goal, however, was not to feed her animal attraction, but to show her the love, labor, and drudgery involved in owning pets.

I had Nicole call the ASPCA to see what kind of volunteer work we could do on weekends, only to find out that volunteers have to be at least fourteen. (I guess this could be a bad news/good news type of thing, eh?) But on a subsequent call we discovered that there were still other ways to help out. They asked Nicole to bring in three things: pet food, old towels and rags, and newspapers rolled into logs (they're easier to roll out in cages this way).

Armed with this list, Nicole and I worked out how she could get these items together. She came up with the following plan: I would help by matching her allowance dollar for dollar (both come out of the same pocket, I might add, for those of you not taking notes). She would then buy cookie ingredients, bake cookies, and then she and I would traverse the neighborhood selling these baked goods. She'd use all the proceeds to buy pet food. At each stop, she would also ask for donations of towels and/or newspapers.

On Friday night, she showed me a thing or two about baking cookies; on Saturday morning, I taught her how to sell door to door. It really was wonderful, watching neighbors' reactions change from a look that said, "Don't disturb me with a sales call on a Saturday morning" to "Oh what a cute/great (depending on the gender of the person answering the door) idea!" Not only did Nicole sell all of her cookies, but she also took orders for several dozen more. I had to switch my manly-man convertible for the family van to pick up all the stacks and stacks of donated newspapers and towels. As we drove to the shelter, I absolutely beamed with pride as I watched my smiling daughter, looking like an absolute angel, so proud of having done what she at first thought would be a boring chore.

This started out as a quick weekend project, but it has turned into something that may last a lifetime. As Nicole saw the excited and appreciative faces when we made our first delivery, she whispered to me that she wanted to rush home and start all over again. Although she wasn't old enough to officially volunteer, the workers let her help around the office a bit. She was also allowed to visit the cat corner, where she spent time petting the current residents. One of the workers took Nicole and me on a special tour and talked at length with her about the care and feeding requirements of all the animals. We also got to hear about all of the pets families dump there because the "cute" had worn off.

It's been months since our initial ASPCA weekend, and Nicole's attitude about her "animal kingdom" has changed dramatically. She has written several compositions for school about what kids can do to better take care of their pets . . . and she even wrote the principal a letter offering to demonstrate the care and feeding of the various classroom pets. She also got her fourth-grade class to take on her Cookies for Pets drive as a class project.

Did we accomplish what we set out to do? Well, my wife still cleans Woody's cage from time to time, but Nicole almost al-

Calling All Animal Lovers!

There are number of things you can do with your pet-loving children:

- Be a volunteer at the zoo. From cleaning to guiding, they need you.
- Train guide dogs for the blind.
- Volunteer at the ASPCA—or deliver items they need, which you can collect: newspapers, blankets, and pet food.
- Walk dogs for elderly neighbors.
- Get involved in saving the rain forests.
- Contribute to the World Wildlife Fund.
- Encourage older kids to intern at a veterinary clinic.
- Become an animal breeder. (Have you ever felt how soft chinchilla fur is?)

ways feeds the animals without having to be prompted. And, yes, she still wants a huge house with a school bus full of animals. But the best part of the whole deal is that I got to spend lots of one-on-one time with my sweet little girl because as we baked cookies, cleaned up the kitchen, sold and delivered cookies, and picked up newspapers and towels we talked and laughed and even held hands. I saw her as I never had before, not just as my little girl, but also as a truly helpful, caring person. Even though I still have to clean the dog run, I know I came out the winner from that weekend.

19

Bike, Schmike— Gimme a Hog!

I've debated with myself for days over whether to write about this particular subject. (I guess if I'm debating with myself, either way it goes, I win, eh?) Anyway, I've decided to go for it. I'm no wuss. Let's do it. Here we go.

Buy your wife flowers each and every day and tell her you love her at least ten times a day.

I just wrote that in case she's reading ahead of you. Once she reads that, she'll turn to you, kiss you, and say, "Darling, you keep on reading and do whatever that nice man suggests you do!" Okay . . . is she gone? Good. All right, men, quietly now. Gather around and let's move on.

The real subject of this chapter is to take your kid on a motorcycle adventure. If you don't own one, you need to beg, borrow, rent, or, er, uh, *buy* one, and head out on the highway, looking for adventure. . . . Everybody sing along: "Born to be wild!"

But first some facts:

Fact: Riding a motorcycle is often dangerous. This is not because of the rider necessarily, but because of automobiles and road kill you might come in contact with.

Fact: When a motorcycle and a car crash together, the motorcycle loses—as does the motorcycle rider(s). (Some hospitals call the machines "donor-cycles.")

Fact: Riding a motorcycle is one of the most exciting things you can do.

If you are fortunate enough to own, rent, or borrow a bike, take your child with you on a ride that the two of you plan together. (Many vacation spots rent out Vespa-type scooters, which are safer—because you can't go as fast—but are still quite a blast.) Teach him (or her!) the safety rules of the road. Start by taking him out for "practice" trips before the big one. Show him how to be a safe passenger, including watching out for the potential "burn spots" (especially that tail pipe!) to avoid. Get helmets, protective clothing, steel-toed boots, gloves, sunglasses—every bit of protection that you can possibly put on him—so that Mom will let you go in the first place. While you're at it, take Mom on one of the planning rides and let her feel the exhilaration of riding a bike with a *real* man (that's you). Hint: This might help smooth over your plan to buy a motorcycle later on.

Head down to the local motorcycle dealership. You'll be blown away. There are many brands to choose from: Yamaha, Triumph, Honda, Suzuki, Kawasaki, Victory, and, of course . . . Harley-Davidson.

Easy Rider

There are ways to experience the feeling of riding a motorcycle without ever really riding one. Most video arcades have games where you sit on a motorcycle simulator. You actually lean into the turns that you see on the video monitor in front of you. This is a very safe way to experience the exhilaration while saving many thousands of dollars at the same time.

As a last resort, go to your area kiddie-land park where they might have a motorcycle-themed merry-go-round. Have your wife ride with you, and maybe, just maybe, she'll be as humiliated as you! If so, don't let her off the ride until she agrees to let you try the real thing.

I was at a financial planning meeting the other day and one of the speakers pointed out that Harley stock is up due to all the baby boomers hitting forty and buying a "Hog." Most of these Hogs are so dressed out by the time they leave the showroom floor that, for another $50, the buyer could have owned a seven-bedroom timeshare in Aspen.

In fact, just the other day I was having a burger at Geneva's (see chapter 28, "The Quest for the Holy Grail of Burgers") with my two older boys when a fiftyish guy with a ponytail pulled up on a Harley the size of a four-door pickup truck. He spent about fifteen minutes getting out of his custom leathers and designer helmet before placing his hamburger order.

As the Harley rider ate, my boys huddled around the highly lacquered, midnight-blue, mega-chromed Harley, stand-

ing a respectful distance away to avoid getting shot for en-
croaching on his machine's territory. Another guy, who looked
about seventeen and wore more silver and chrome on his body
and clothing than there was on the Harley in front of him,
stopped dead in his tracks. He stared at the bike for a long moment, then turned his gaze to Mr. Ponytail. He couldn't have
looked more stunned than if he had seen the pope sitting there
having a double-cheese bacon-avocado burger. Not taking his
eyes off the boomer, he whispered reverently, "Nice bike man.
I'm serious, nice bleepin' bike," then turned and meandered
away. Mr. Ponytail never blinked, gulped down his last chunk
of burger, sucked up his last drop of piña colada milk shake,
spent another fifteen minutes pulling on his leathers and helmet, and mounted his stallion. A push of a button and he was
gone. Who was that masked man?

My boys and I knew that the Harley store was just around
the corner, so we dropped in. If you visit a Harley dealership
yourself, don't go expecting a grungy old motorcycle shop. This
place was incredible: Millions of dollars' worth of bikes sat
sparkling on the floor near racks and racks of enough acces-
sories to bankrupt the sultan of Brunei. You can buy a Softail,
Night Train, Fat Boy, Road King, Dyna Glide (available in low
rider), or, if you can find one in stock, the awesome-looking
V-Rod for $20,000 to $25,000, depending on how decked out
you want it to be. And that's just for the bike.

Financial commitments aside, riding a motorcycle with
your kid will be an unforgettable experience—if you are super
careful. Never expect anyone but you to follow the rules of the
road. Expect the unexpected. I owned a bike once long ago. I

used to ride through the countryside, inhaling the scents of chimney smoke and new-mown hay, bugs in my teeth. I had a Honda 750 with about every extra you could buy, not unlike Mr. Ponytail at Geneva's. The day I decided to rethink motorcycle ownership, I was driving down a main street of town wearing my full dress leathers when a bleary-eyed, scraggly-bearded jerk in a rusted-out, beat-up excuse for a pickup truck ran me off of the road, gesturing at me in that *special* way, questioning the legitimacy of my birth, and calling me a "hippie." That last one really hurt. I sold the bike after that, but I sure do miss it.

Remember the old guy on *Hill Street Blues* who always said, at the end of roll call, as the cops were heading out to their beats, "Be careful out there"? Do!

And now, we return to the part that your wife can read:

So remember, men: Buy your wife flowers every day and tell her you love her ten times a day. Take her out to dinner, often. And remember, she's always right! (Hey guys, it's for a Harley, okay?)

20

Yo-Yo Pa

Talk about your "oldie but goodie," here's a fun activity that can start on a weekend, but will more than likely become an everyday obsession. Teach your child to yo-yo! Now, although this may seem like a rather pedestrian thing to do, I'll tell you about some yo-yo tricks later that will have your yo-yo—and your head—spinning.

First, some history on this round whirling mound. Where was the first yo-yo produced? No one knows for sure, but it's thought to have come from either Greece or China around 500 B.C. Some of the first yo-yos were made of wood or metal; some decorative ones were even made of terra cotta. Throughout history, whether in Peking, Paris, or the Philippines, there are stories about the mystery of the yo-yo. Whether it was called a disc, a *bandalore, l'emigrette,* or the romantic-sounding *joujou de Normandie,* I'm sure that from the first, it thrilled its users as they successfully flipped, spun, and retracted it without bopping themselves in the nose.

I've read that Stone Age hunters may have used a type of yo-yo, perhaps a stone with a hole in its middle and a string wrapped around it, to kill animals. The hunter positioned himself in a tree, threw the stone, then jerked it back after the attack. In 1815, Napoleon supposedly relaxed by playing with a yo-yo before the Battle of Waterloo. The yo-yo has even been in space. In 1985 and again in 1992, astronauts used a yo-yo to test gravitational pull. They discovered that the yo-yo wouldn't drop, of course, and instead they had to thrust it forward. And they couldn't do the one trick that everyone who has ever played with a yo-yo has tried: The yo-yo couldn't "sleep" in space—that is, it couldn't spin continuously. (I'll teach you how to do this one later, then you can teach your kids how to do it.) Without the downward pull of gravity, the yo-yo went as far as its string allowed, then headed right back up.

The yo-yo became a yo-yo (said to be the Filipino word meaning "come-come" or "to return") in the late 1900s when Donald Duncan saw a man doing yo-yo tricks on a street corner in San Francisco. Recognizing a money-making opportunity, Duncan turned the little wooden orb into a multimillion-dollar business, patenting the name "yo-yo," and eventually giving the Duncan yo-yo worldwide recognition. But in 1965, the patent was rescinded because the name yo-yo was now synonymous with the toy itself. Duncan's empire eventually crumbled, but the yo-yo goes on.

The best way to get started with your weekend of ups and downs (and round and rounds!) is to hit the Internet. Check out the American Yo-Yo Association's site at www.ayya.net and you'll find a treasure trove of information (including much of the historical data I've mentioned here). There is a listing for yo-yo clubs from Hawaii to Canada, California to Rhode Island. There are even contests in many states to test yo-yoers' skills. I was surprised to see DeRidder, Louisiana, the tiny town mentioned in chapter 21, as the site for the Louisiana yo-yo championships.

By the way, if you think your choices in yo-yos are limited to those cheapo little pieces of wood glued together or even cheaper lightweight plastic models, check out the latest models, which come with centrifugal-spring transaxles and ball-bearing axles for longer spin times.

I found a yo-yo with a little how-to booklet attached at the local science museum. The basic tricks are tons of fun and will eat up most of your day. Here are a few "getting started" tips so you can pretend to know more than your kid does:

First, wind the yo-yo by holding it with one hand while pinching the string a few inches above the yo-yo with the other. Wind three or four turns loosely, hand over hand. As your fingers move closer to the body of the yo-yo, pull the string sideways to tighten it up. For your first toss, turn your palm face up, yo-yo in it, and then pull your arm toward your chest, snapping your wrist forward and down, making your yo-yo go-go. If you have wound the string correctly, as the yo-yo hits the bottom of the string it will spin. Announce to your child in your most authoritative voice, "My yo-yo is now sleeping," then flick your wrist upward, bringing baby back home to papa. (If it doesn't sleep that means the string is too tight.)

My favorite trick is "walking the dog." (It's so simple, even I can do it. That's why it's my favorite.) When the yo-yo hits

Lego My Yo-yo

If you want to start moving toward the more radical side of the art of yo-yo, check out the names of some of the moves required at sanctioned competitions. Each age group has its own level of difficulty.

Eight and Under:
Gravity Pull
Throw-down
One Outside Loop

Novices and Juniors:
Walk the Dog
Hop the Fence
Loop the Loop

Seniors and Up:
Buddha's Revenge
Brain Twister with Two Somersaults and a Skin the Cat Dismount
Warp Drive (Loop the Loop to Around the World— three times!)
Double or Nothing with an Upward Toss or Rolling Upward Toss Dismount

Listen to the names of these other maneuvers: Dizzy Baby, Boingy Boingy, Cold Fusion, Kwijibo, Iron Whip, and, of course, Suicide.

And as if these contortions weren't enough, as you're performing the judges are also watching:

- Elegance of yo-yo control

- Smoothness of the yo-yo's line of trajectory

- Movement while yo-yoing and use of yo-yo space

- Amplitude and maturity of yo-yo maneuvers

- Speed control

- Stage presence and choreography (while performing more difficult tricks) the sleeper position, slowly lower it to a surface and let it "walk" as you walk with it. Don't let your doggy die, though. Flick it back up if your pup starts to poop out.

Now let's "loop the loop." Throw the yo-yo out in front of you, underhand, and as the yo-yo reaches its spin zone directly in front of you, pull it back to you, ducking your hand underneath each time it reaches your string finger. You're doing it! Exciting, eh?

When you go online to do your yo-yo research, be sure to find out where the yo-yo clubs in your area hold meetings or demonstrations. Many of them get together during their lunch hour each week just to share stories and entertain yo-yo amateurs like us.

If you start with the basic premise that you and your child are just going to have some fun finding out if you can make this ancient toy go, that in itself will make for a fun day. After all is said and done—contests won and contests lost, incredible tricks performed making the yo-yo dance, flying through the air with the greatest of ease, and defy gravity—we beginners are still not so different from the professionals. In the end, one is judged on whether the yo-yo ends as it began, fully rewound and in your hand. We can do that, can't we?

Happy yo-yoing!

21

On the Road Again

So, who am I writing about in this chapter? Jack Kerouac? Maybe Willie Nelson? How about a remake of the *Dukes of Hazard*? Nope, none of the above. "Old Man" Hal Albertson inspired this chapter.

I was conferring with my younger son the other day (if one can indeed *confer* with a thirteen-year-old) when the subject of his Eagle Scout project came up. We talked about duck shelters, park benches for the elderly, cleaning and restoring headstones and graves at historic cemeteries, and so on. The more we talked, the less interested he seemed to be in those ideas. That's when I told him about Hal.

Hal Albertson is the inspiration for a great weekend activity for you and one or more of your children. The time shared together will be productive, fun, challenging, and perhaps even a little entertaining. But first I need to give you a little background on Hal.

I met Hal via the telephone when he called me at the television station where I anchored the news and hosted a commu-
nity-service program. He called to gripe about the conditions
of society in general, and Sacramento's roadsides in particular.
Hal founded, runs, and is the living symbol for CIMBL (Citizens Involved for Better Living). I met Hal in person when he
agreed to appear on my program.

Hal Albertson is a crusty, weather-worn, three-pack-a-
day, seventy-year-old ball of coughing energy who won't take
no for an answer. I know, I tried many times. As a young
man, Hal worked for Aerojet in the general nucleonics division designing nuclear reactors for a cleaner, better, nuclear-
powered America. Ten years later, he was out of a job. He
tried his hand as an inventor, coming close with two ideas.
One was a prototype for what today is a very common thing:
a way to enclose your outdoor patio using lightweight, inexpensive materials. The problem with his method, he says, was
that he couldn't get the cost down to a profitable margin. His
other near bump with success had to do with, in his words,
pumping the "ooze from the bottom of the ocean" to feed the
plankton above, all for the purpose of feeding the protein-
poor of the world. His heart was in the right place, but once
again, he didn't have the capital to move forward. He passed
his idea along to the World Health Organization, and now
thirty-odd years later, Hal's still wondering what happened to
the idea. When his career as an inventor didn't work out, he
got a job working on the county's roads by day, he took classes
at night, and eventually got a degree in business. He became

a certified financial planner and did well enough to retire in 1989. And then he went to work.

Hal formed CIMBL because he was "ticked off" about the direction our country is headed. He believes the only way to save America is to fight back against the cancers that are killing our society: teen violence, drunk driving, drugs, gangs . . . even litter. He wants us to involve ourselves in society—help staff the library, assist at the police department, and help out at church, the chamber of commerce, retirement homes—wherever help is needed.

Hal's two favorite hot buttons are drunk drivers and litter. With regard to the first, he suggests that if you see one and don't report him or her, you are then somewhat responsible for the drunk driver's actions. Call 911 and report the incident. You could be a hero.

With regard to litter, this is where CIMBL comes in. Hal formed the organization back in 1994 as a way to "get done whatever needed to be done in our community." His initial membership consisted of . . . Hal Albertson. Now it is more than 400 strong, with new members joining as they hear about it. High school students are even forming chapters after they've spent a day on the road with CIMBL, which has assisted with the cleanup following two floods that hit the area. CIMBL volunteers filled sandbags and sorted donated clothing and food. They have organized food and clothing drives for earthquake-stricken areas and even helped in an after-school tutoring program. But CIMBL's main goal is getting rid of litter. (I remember, as a child, seeing a sign from the back seat of the family car as we passed through the town of

Delitter Your Own Hometown

So, how can you and yours get involved if you don't live in this area? I asked Hal that very question, and here's what he said: "Call me!"

He's serious: Call him. He can tell you who to approach to join or form your own community group. He'll tell you how to get the trash bags, the brightly colored safety vests for roadside work, even the fancy pickup sticks with the "grabbers" that save wear and tear on your back.

Oh, and you might want to call in the evening or on the weekend, when long-distance rates are low, as Hal "believes strongly in what he's doing." Translation: Hal's a talker.

Here's a quick list of things you'll need to get started on your own community-improvement program:

- Support from your county board of supervisors and/or city council
- Volunteers
- Refreshments (Hal has great suggestions on how to get these for free)
- Volunteers
- A truck
- Volunteers
- A good pair of walking shoes and a hat
- Volunteers
- Cleanup equipment
- A liability release form for each volunteer to sign

Contact: Hal Albertson
1290 Monument Place
Newcastle, CA 95658
(916) 642-3599

DeRidder, Louisiana. It read: "De-Litter DeRidder." Okay, so some memories aren't as earth-shaking as others.)

CIMBL volunteers have delittered more than 2,000 miles of roads, removing more than 20,000 big black bags full of trash. The group has also removed items like washing machines, TVs, refrigerators, couches . . . and more than 1,600 tires. Some of the more unusual items recovered: a wallet with $250 in cash, a huge case of new auto parts, a complete automobile transmission, a bag of U.S. mail apparently stolen off of a delivery truck, and a complete and intact telephone booth—intact, that is, except for the coin box. The only thing CIMBL volunteers haven't come across yet—though Hal worries they will one day—is a body. He says he mentions this possibility to each group during his pre-delitter pep talk. Last month, just prior to a scheduled cleanup, a body was discovered on the group's original planned route. Fortunately, the route had been changed the week before.

CIMBL has been honored for its work by the County of Placer, the State of California, the cities of Lincoln, Auburn, and Loomis—and even the White House. The message and motto of CIMBL is: "Whatever the community needs, we will do it!"

What a great message—and what a great way to spend time with your child while you give back something to your community. (For info on how to start a community-improvement group in your own area, see "Delitter Your Own Hometown," page 105.) You and your kids can do your civic duty and have an adventure at the same time. When I met with Hal to get some of the information for this chapter, I told him that I'd make sure he got a copy of the book in exchange for all of his input. He coughed, as he lit another of his charcoal-filtered death sticks, laughed a lung-rattling laugh, and speculated that he might not be around by then, owing to his emphysema and all.

He's such an ornery cuss.

But he can teach us all a valuable lesson: Get involved with your community. You might even consider getting your child's entire school involved. No matter where you live, all you need to do is pick up the phone and give Hal a call. He's got the whole system down to a science and he's more than willing to share his knowledge—for free—with you and your children (see "Delitter Your Own Hometown" for his contact info). He's even got a contingency plan in the event that his tobacco addiction proves stronger than his conviction. Even if he can no longer answer, someone will. Call Hal. Tell him that you and your children want to get involved in helping America become what we all know it should be. Tell him you want to teach your children and your community about better living through involved citizens.

Then tell him to quit smoking. Tell him that CIMBL really stands for: "Cigarettes Inhaled Means Burned Lungs."

Come on, Hal. Throw, the butts away. We love you . . . and there are still too many DeRidders to delitter.

22

This One Is for the Birds

Don't knock this activity if you haven't tried it. I'm suggesting you learn the art of bird watching with your kids this weekend. If you think it's not for you, I would be willing to bet that at least once in your life, you have stopped to admire a hummingbird, or watched a flock of Canada geese flying low in formation, or been intrigued by a woodpecker banging his head against a tree (not unlike how we feel some days at work, eh?). Pick a bird, any bird; you'll find things to admire about it. (I'm referring, of course, to birds in the wild, not caged birds that mess up the carpets with seed husks and such.)

So let's go bird watching. In researching this, I discovered that over the next hundred years or so, we will lose more than 1,000 bird species to extinction. How can being a bird watcher help stop this loss? If we teach our children about our responsibility to protect our planet, they too will teach the generations to come. Wouldn't it be a wonderful legacy to know that your great-great-grandchildren are able to enjoy the beauty of nature because of something *you* did with your own kids?

Let's begin. As always, the Web is loaded with information. Type *bird watching* into your favorite search engine and you're set. The National Audubon Society's site, for example, blew me away (www.audubon.org).

The basic guidelines for bird watching are: protect nature and buy a really great set of binoculars. Don't have the binoculars? Just type *binoculars* in your search engine and you'll find whatever you need to know to make the purchase. I found Bushnell's 80×40 Birder Binoculars for $75, Bausch and Lomb's 80×42 Elite for $1,800, or you can hike all the way up to the top of the mountain and get Zeiss 20×60 Image Stabilized binoculars for the bargain price of only $4,867. (Actually, until you're sure this is going to turn into a lifetime type of hobby, it's probably best to borrow a pair from a sports-nut friend of yours.)

Now you're ready to go, but where is the best location? Check with your local nature center, Audubon Society, or bird club. Check the yellow pages under, you guessed it, *Birds*. The state and national park services can also be of service, giving you advice not only about where to go but also what to look for.

As you and your children get into this, you might even want to make your yard into a more "bird-friendly" place. Consider adding places for birds to drink and bathe. Whether you build a birdbath, pond, or just set out a water dish, it should be no more than two inches deep. This allows the birds to play, bathe, and drink safely. Speaking of safety, it's best to put their water source up off the ground several feet to give the birds a better view of any predators that might be lurking about. A place for the birds to hide is also a good idea. Plant some shrubs or evergreen trees that they can escape to, if necessary.

You also need to consider food sources. You and the birds can both benefit here. Plant some fruit trees or flowering plants for your eyes and their little bellies. They also love oak, hickory, and maple trees.

As you spend time bird watching with your children, in nature or in your own backyard, you'll also want to share with them the code of ethics put together by the American Birding Association (www.americanbirding.org). I won't write out the entire list, but here are some of the highlights:

- ★ Do not disturb the birds in any way.
- ★ Avoid chasing or repeatedly flushing the birds.
- ★ Keep an appropriate distance from nests and nesting colonies.
- ★ Refrain from handling birds or eggs unless engaged in recognized research activities.
- ★ Leave the habitat the way you find it.
- ★ Respect the privacy and property of others by observing "No Trespassing" signs.
- ★ Assume responsibility for the conduct of the group.
- ★ Limit groups to a size that does not threaten the environment or the peace and tranquility of others.

Have a wonderful lifetime of weekends in nature with your children. This is one of the greatest gifts you can give them.

Build the Perfect Birdhouse

A trip to your local library or bookstore will help a lot with this activity. There are several publications, such as *Wild Bird, Birder's World, Bird Times,* and *Bird Watcher's Digest,* with articles, information, and pictures of birds specific to your area.

I was surprised at the variety of birdhouses there are. Each bird has its own specific housing requirements (although I don't know what the penalty is if one bird is caught moving in to another bird's house), such as:

Tufted Titmouse Birdhouse

Floor size	4 inches square
Depth	8 to 10 inches
Entrance height	6 to 8 inches above the floor
Entrance diameter	1¼ inches
Above-ground height	6 to 15 feet

Redheaded Woodpecker Penthouse

Floor size	6 inches square
Depth	1 foot
Entrance height	10 inches above the floor
Entrance diameter	2 inches
Above-ground height	10 to 20 feet

For more information on different types of birdhouses, as well as step-by-step instructions on building one, see the U.S. Fish and Wildlife Web site (http://migratorybirds .fws.gov).

23

Be Alert!

(The World Needs More Lerts)

This chapter has to do with teaching your child to write. Now, don't be afraid, we're not talking about sonnets or novels here. I'm only talking about teaching your child about communicating feelings and love through words.

The title of this chapter comes from one of my wife's memories of her father. He had a habit of leaving short, funny notes for her to find. In this case, he left on her pillow a note with "Be Alert!" written on it, and an arrow pointing to the edge of the paper. When she flipped the piece of paper over, the rest of the note said, "The world needs more lerts!" Another time he left a note on her pillow reading, "Turn me over!" On the other side he had written, "Ah, that feels better!" Knowing my wife, a precocious little towhead, she probably groaned a little and said, "Oh, Dad!"—the same way my kids say it to me!—every time he left her one of his notes. But as she reflects on the notes now, long after her father passed away, it's with fondness and affection.

A great way to start this bonding activity is with, of course, food. I love to pack my kids' school lunches and enclose in each innocent brown paper bag some sort of note, riddle, poem, joke, or even a toy that will brighten their day. For about two weeks running, I put weird stuff in my thirteen-year-old son's lunch bag. One day it was a small lightbulb, another it was a doggy chew, then a sponge. I even put in some fake cat poop that his older brother had brought home as a joke. My son acted more frustrated each time, laughing and begging me to stop. But he secretly admitted to his mom that he and his friends howled over his surprises every day at lunch. Each morning he'd undertake an inspection of his lunch bag, trying to catch me in the act. Once I opened an individual package of chocolate chip cookies, took out the end ones, put in an ugly rubber spiked toy and resealed the package. I could tell he was impressed when he came home ranting, raving, and laughing about the discovery. At that point, I told him that I was only going to do this twice more, the next two days, and then the great brown bag mystery tour would be over. On the next to last day, I put nothing in his lunch bag, letting him go bonkers searching through everything before we left for school, knowing there would be something, but coming up empty handed. Then, when he went out to load his bike onto the car's bike rack, I slipped a huge doggy pull toy, the kind with a rope on one end and a gigantic, bright yellow plastic ball on the other end, into his back pack with the rope part wrapped around his lunch bag. I heard about that one for weeks.

On the final day, I didn't put anything in his lunch, but I *did* write a note on his napkin and folded it so he wouldn't see

Play on Words

Another way you can encourage your children to experiment with words and writing—and have some together time—is to write a story together. You can do it the way I suggest in this chapter—you transcribing as your child makes up the story. Or you can write it together.

Suggest to your child that you write a story together. If she goes for it, explain how it will work. She'll start the story with the first sentence (or first paragraph, if you prefer). Then she'll hand it off to you. You read what she's written, write another sentence, then hand it back to her. You can decide up front how long it will be or agree on the end point together. The idea is to be as wild and creative as possible—to one-up each other and have fun at the same time.

You can make this even more fun by covering up what each person has written, except for one visible line of words. Each person has to write the next bit with just a few words of the other person's last contribution—which makes for a pretty wacky story when you unfold the piece of paper and read the story out loud at the end.

Another way to encourage a love of language is to play word games such as Scrabble, Balderdash, or even that old standby: hangman (see chapter 30, "Get Your Head in the Game").

the note until he unfolded the napkin. On the note I wrote the silliest poem about what fun this had been, ending with "And now that it's over, you'll pretend to be glad, but now you face each day with no reason to lament, 'Oh, Dad!'" I have now switched my tactics completely by leaving him a note of encouragement each day, telling him how proud of him I am. He likes these new notes, but I can tell that, secretly, he misses the hunt.

Notes are also a great way to spur a later discussion about the meaning of your words, or a chance to watch them work through a riddle you've given them, with your help. This is also great way to encourage a child who's having a tough time with a particular area in his life—school, friends, sports, or whatever.

I like the idea of working with a child on storytelling or poetry. (Don't panic at the word "poetry." It's not as tough as it seems.) Teachers often assign stories as homework assignments, asking the kids to tie them in to the subject being covered in class. Spending some time to show them how to develop a storyline or main idea will not only give you time together, but it might also help bring their grades up a notch. The best way to get them interested in storytelling is either by reading together or making up stories together. (This should start as early as possible!) When children are very young, they love stories of all kinds. As they get older, we often forget the fun we had together at story time. Revisit that activity, only this time have *them* be the storytellers while you write it down, or have them write the story and then read it to you. Get their minds percolating with ideas, scenes, and descriptions—and watch them take off.

Poetry can be fun, too. You can introduce them to the cleverness of, say, an Ogden Nash, or the wackiness of a Shel Silverstein, or take the high road and read them about love and nature. Or you can show them how they can be their own favorite poet. You make up one line, then they follow with a line that rhymes, and so on. You're welcome to make up the silliest combination of words and phrases, and although it may not be recognized by any Pulitzer committee, it will be a source of many "yuks" for you and your child, guaranteed!

In fact, I think "napkin poetry" should be recognized as a separate category in poetry competitions. I wish I'd saved the hundreds and hundreds I've sent to school with my unsuspecting children—notes that they most likely filed in some unappreciative landfill somewhere. Save yours. Put them in a box someplace. I cannot imagine the joy you, your child, and, later, their own children will feel revisiting these wonderful examples of your bond with your kids.

Letters, notes, poems—whatever words you share with your children make a connection with them, even when you're not there. My wife's father wrote notes and left them for her to discover while he was at work or on a trip. Can you imagine how much it would mean to your child if you left her a note telling her that, while you're away, she could play detective, looking for other notes that you had hidden for her? You could even make each note a clue that leads her to the hiding place of the next note. The quest itself will be etched in your child's memory of happy times, rather than sadness or resentment about your absence on "another" business trip.

And what goes around, comes around. What dad wouldn't love to carry in his wallet a little note that reads:

Dear Daddy,
I love you.
And I no
You love me to.

See, didn't I tell you not to be afraid of poetry? Write with your children. Write now.

24

Hey, Hey, We're the Monkeys

Sometimes, spending time alone with your child just doesn't work out. So you drop back ten yards and punt. You do what you have to do. How about spending time this weekend with your kid and some of his buddies . . . all dressed as gorillas? Make that gorillas with swords.

Initially I intended this chapter to focus on taking your child on a tour of sorts of your city. The idea here is to find the tallest building (or a very tall parking structure) in town, go to the top of the building (as long as it's publicly accessible) so you can look out over the cityscape, and teach your child a little geography from a hawk's-eye view. This will help give him a greater perspective on the place where you live.

Now, even though my attempt at sharing this activity with my son didn't quite work out as planned, this is still a great activity. You might even consider looking in the yellow pages under *Private Aircraft* to find out how much it would cost to hire a pilot to fly you and your child over the city for a few hours. I had the opportunity to do this in a company helicopter. My son and I had a ball trying to point out his school, our church, our house. It also gave us a different perspective on how the streets interconnect around our neighborhood.

But what's that old saying about "the best-laid plans of mice and men"?

I had planned this excursion with my son a few days in advance, but, when I reminded him on the morning of the appointed afternoon, his face was blank. He had completely forgotten about it. It seems he was totally absorbed in his French class final project and all else had fallen by the wayside. He was a little embarrassed and, at first, asked if we could do our tour next week, or even later. Then, after a moment, his eyes went wild, his brain started smoking, and he shouted, "Wait, let's do it today!"

I should have known something was up, but, we foolish pops, we never learn. Innocently, I went along with his plan. I was to meet him at our house after school and from there we would head to town.

When I pulled into my driveway, I noticed there were several cars parked in front of the house, but I didn't pay much attention. I opened the front door . . . and had to force my way in through the crowd. There were guys of every size and shape, all classmates of my son, yelling, laughing, talking, and answering each other, all at the same time. They were waving some ghastly black fabric about, and several other boys were messing with my son's sword collection. Still, my radar hadn't registered danger signals yet. I doubt that even the "Men in Black" would have been prepared for what was yet to come.

My son asked if I could drive his group downtown to the building I was going to show him and I said, "Sure!" When I brought the van around and honked the horn, out came three guys dressed in gorilla suits, one guy with a video camera, another with a boom microphone, and the last one yelling instructions to the others while he carried several of the swords.

I finally realized this was not going to be your ordinary trip downtown in the minivan. I asked what was going on and they revealed their plan.

They wanted me to take them to our town's tallest building so they could shoot their class project about three gorillas that take over the world—in French, of course. I'm still not quite sure exactly where they got the idea for the plot, but imagine trying to explain to a parking lot attendant who spoke very little English and absolutely no French what it was these kids wanted to do on his roof. Actually, I didn't have to do much explaining: He just handed me the ticket and waved us onward and upward, looking for all the world as though he saw a minivan full of boys in gorilla suits every day.

Once on the roof of the garage, I began pointing out to my young audience the various buildings, highways, and rivers, as well as the new minor-league baseball stadium and other landmarks in our fair city. Of course, when I turned around, I realized that not a single soul had heard a word I'd said. The "director" started shouting stuff to the "actors," and the "videographer" began his *cinema verite*. The clowns in gorilla suits bounced around, running and thrusting swords at each other— basically going berserk—in French, of course. Two chased one,

Get Your Bearings

The first rule in sharing geography with your children is, of course, making sure they know how to read maps. The most practical way to start is to find about where your house is on a map of your city, mark it with a big red X, and then work with them to find other landmarks—like your favorite park, your children's schools, friends' and relatives' homes, and so on. Be sure to teach—and rein-force!—the use of directions, that is, north, south, east, and west, rather than just left, right, or catty-corner. When you're out and about, make a game of figuring out which direction you're headed, and if you're ever lost to-gether, let your child in on figuring out how to get back on track. (Here's a tip: If you're a member of the Ameri-can Automobile Association, you can get city and state maps for free! Stock up on the most current maps of your area and share them with your children.)

If you can't arrange a plane or helicopter ride over your city, you can head to the library together to look at aerial maps of the area. Throw in a little bit of history by looking at maps from different eras.

then one chased two. I had no idea which one was my son, and I was getting to the point where I didn't really care.

I could only imagine what anyone in an office with a view of these goings-on thought of the chaos being enacted there. I shouted out to my simian son that I would leave them to their shooting and that they should call me when they needed a ride home, figuring that when I came back I'd take them out for ice cream and get the recap of the day's shoot.

As the afternoon progressed into evening, I got busy doing other things and forgot about the *Planet of the Apes* wannabes for a while. A call to my son's cell phone failed to reach him. I guess gorillas don't have pockets. Around 7:00 that evening, I began to get worried, so I told the saner members of my family to call me if they heard from Cheeta.

I was just driving into the downtown area when my phone started buzzing, so I grabbed it, flipped it open, and heard on the other end: "Dad, could you come pick us up? We're being detained by the CHP security at the state Capitol. Come to the security area—and bring your identification." I was too shaken up to ask anything other than if he was okay, to which he answered with a chuckle, "Yeah, *we* are, but I'm not sure about the security guys."

I arrived at the well-lighted Capitol building and hurriedly went to the appointed spot. An officer met me at the security window, made me prove my identity, and then let me in to a small, dimly lit room where a chagrined group of teenage actors waited, happy to see an adult who was on their side, or at least an adult they *hoped* would be. And I was. I vouched for their integrity, if not their sanity, and the officers decided they would not press any charges *if* the boys promised not to do *that* again. I decided to wait until we were off the Capitol grounds to make them tell me what *that* was supposed to mean.

It seems that the boys had spent all afternoon shooting at the parking garage. Then they left and proceeded to get kicked out of a couple of restaurants when they tried to order something to drink, in costume—in French, of course. They were able to find a few friendly tourists who thought it cute to take their picture on the Capitol grounds with the "dueling gorillas." As it began to get dark, the boys decided to head to the rotunda of the Capitol building, thinking what a great shot that would make. Did they ask permission? No. Did they just head right up and start taping, swords and all? Yes, of course they did.

They found out later that the security cameras picked them up as they were beginning to jump, shout, and sword fight . . . in French, of course. Later, the boys just about busted a gut imagining what the officer in the security control room said to alert the four officers who responded to this "emergency."

"Ed, call the other guys. There are some giant monkeys having a sword fight on the third level of the rotunda. And they're all yelling at each other . . . in French."

The boys have chutzpah. They even asked if they could have a copy of the security video footage, particularly the part where the officers arrived and shouted out in a loud voice, not sure if they would understand him: "Take off the monkey suits and put your swords down." The CHP captain declined.

We later had a movie premiere party at our house to watch the film (and I still didn't understand a word of it). But the guys ran, reran, and ran again the shot that their school camera *did* catch. Turns out the scared cameraman continued to roll the tape as the officers cautiously approached, hands on holsters. Re-watching the tape, the boys howled every time the very puzzled lead officer shouted, "Take off the monkey suits—" and they'd yell in unison, "Gorillas!" as if watching *Mystery Science Theatre 3000*. They'd yell, cheer, and high-five one another as the officer's hand covered up the lens of the camera, just like they do in the movies.

I gave up trying to explain how this really could have been a huge problem and how lucky the boys were to get off with just a warning. Fortunately for them, this was all before the post–September 11 security craze. They knew they were in the wrong, they knew that I knew they were in the wrong, but— what the heck—after about the tenth time, I decided to join in and shout, "Gorillas!" along with them. It's a memory that none of us will soon forget.

Try a little geography lesson with your child. You just never know what lessons await *you*. But if the kids starting monkeying around . . . take 'em to the movies instead.

25

Oh! I Have Slipped the Surly Bonds of Earth

I have a friend who lives and breathes flying. To say that she is a nut about airplanes would be a gross understatement. A few months back she began to besiege us with info about the Young Eagles program and getting my children involved in it . . . so, choosing between her constant "encouragement" and trying it out, I decided the easier route was to head to the airfield. I really didn't have a firm grasp on what this program was all about, but I figured humoring her was the easiest flight pattern.

I persuaded all four children to go with me, promising them that it would be fun, while inwardly praying that I wasn't telling them a whopper. I kept asking myself, "Self, is there really *any* activity that can equally please and appease ages eight through eighteen?" Turns out, the answer is yes.

What we found when we got there were more spectacular-looking aircraft than I ever could have imagined. The main group sponsoring Young Eagles is the Experimental Aircraft Association (EAA). The folks putting on this gathering were part of a group of more than 22,000 volunteer pilots and others nationwide who serve as the ground crews and helpers. The program's purpose is to take kids flying, for free, to teach them about and encourage them to pursue aviation. So far, this program has given more than 1 million young boys and girls the chance to get their hands on the cockpit controls—that's right, actually flying a plane—for free.

My kids, all four of them, were stoked. Each one got to go up and man the controls. I went along with each of my two youngest and watched as their fear turned to exhilaration and confidence. As my daughter flew, barely able to see over the controls, she kept yelling into the headset, "Daddy, look, I'm turning the plane. Daddy, look I'm flying. Daddy, look I'm—" and on and on. It was great, except for the fact that both the pilot and I had headsets on, and her yelling was cute but painful.

The pilots flying that day were remarkable. There were four times as many kids as there were planes, but these men and women flew flight after flight with nary a complaint, all the while answering the kids' questions and patiently pointing out the same sights over and over. The pilots volunteer their services and aircraft, plus pay for gas so kids from every economic background can have the opportunity to fly. In fact, when EAA went looking for someone to be the program's point man, they got the real "top gun" for the job: Chuck Yeager, the first man to fly faster than the speed of sound.

What a fun day we *all* had. Since then, one son has been studying tapes about flying, and the other three kids can't wait to go back again.

Ready for Takeoff

Here's how to take flight with *your* children. First stop, the Experimental Aircraft Association's Web site: www.eaa.org. (You can also go directly to www.young eagles.org.) You'll find all the information you need about Young Eagles flight dates in your area, plus information on summer aviation camps. Or, if you don't want to wait for the computer to boot up, call this toll-free number: (877) 806-8902. This service will give you the name of the pilot nearest you who can take you and your children up, and will answer questions you might have about becoming a member of the association.

In the course of surfing the Young Eagles site, I noticed an icon labeled "Check out the World's Largest Logbook" and clicked on it. It turned out to be a listing of the name of every child who has ever been a part of the Young Eagles program. I immediately tested it out. I typed in my daughter's name and within seconds, up popped her name, the date she flew, the type of aircraft she flew, and the name of her pilot. It also offers, at the click of a button, a printable certificate of this memory. As I read my children's names, I could feel the warmth of the sun coming in through the plane's windows, and my ears burned as I remembered my daughter's exclamations of joy.

I would normally have ended this chapter here, but I want to point you to the most perfect description of what flying means to the people who love it: a poem called "High Flight." It was written by John Gillespie Magee, Jr., an American who flew for the Royal Canadian Air Force. In September 1941, he composed the poem while flying his Spitfire at 30,000 feet on a high-altitude test flight, finishing just after he touched down. He later sent a copy of these revelations to his parents. On December 11, 1941, Officer Pilot Magee crashed over England. The nineteen-year-old fighter pilot was killed trying to eject from his damaged craft.

You may have heard a portion of this poem before, but read it now with the vision of a child flying by your side for the very first time. If you type "High Flight" into your Internet search engine, you will find numerous links to this wonderful poem, a testament to the great emotions it stirs in so many people. Read the poem; you'll understand.

26

Snoopy, Spiderman, The Boondocks, and Zits

Today is Sunday, which besides being "go to church day" means it's "read the Sunday comics" day. Here's an activity you can do sitting around in your robe, over breakfast, even over the phone if you're a long-distance dad. Read the comics to your kids. This is a tradition your kids will remember their entire lives and will probably carry on with their own kids.

The comics you read should match the age and imagination of your child. Some comics, like "Dilbert," might appeal to older children but might require some explaining to the younger ones. "Peanuts" is a no-brainer . . . but still funny. Newer comics, like "The Boondocks," might sometimes give you pause, but the artist, Aaron McGruder, does make you stop and think. His theme of two young black children living with their rascally grandfather in an upscale, predominately white neighborhood after moving there from "the 'hood" hits all the points on the emotion scales. This comic in particular will give you and your children a lot to discuss, and it offers you a chance to talk with your children about cultures, ethnic backgrounds, and neighborhoods that might be different from their own.

Personally, I dig "Spiderman," but the one comic that has helped me understand my teenagers the most is "Zits." I sincerely mean that. Jerry Scott and Jim Borgman have the teen/family situation down pat. There have been times that I have actually been confounded by my two older sons' actions, until I see Jeremy, the fifteen-year-old main character of the comic, do the same thing. The difference here is that the cartoon depicts *both* sides of the situation . . . and hits the mark right on. Check out "Zits" for a few days before you decide to share it with your teenager.

By the way, this chapter idea sprang from one of my more unusual jobs. After moving from Lake Charles to Lafayette to attend college at the University of Southwestern Louisiana (voted the Number 1 party school in America the years I attended), I got a job as a weekend DJ at an "easy listening" radio station. Part of my weekend shift was to sign the station on Sunday mornings at 6:00 and play music until 8:00. From 8:00 to 9:00 A.M., I became "Uncle Bobby with your Sunday-morning comics, live and on the air." I pretty much just opened the comics and read each one over the air, describing each panel to the listener. (Though I may be acting a bit presumptuous to believe there were actually any listeners. There weren't any sponsors, so that should have been my first clue.)

Head out on a picnic, go to the park, sit on the sofa together. . . . It doesn't matter where or how you do this activity.

Start off by asking them about their favorite comic strip—what is it and why do they like it? Don't judge their choices.

Remember, it's *their* choice. Discuss the cartoon and its social commentary, sarcasm, or just plain silliness. Tell them about your favorite comics when you were a kid and what you like now. Talk about the way the different artists draw their characters. There is enough material in the Sunday comics pages to spend several days talking with your children. Plus, every day in the daily comics there are laughs to share and situations to discuss. Before you know it, it's Sunday comics day again.

Trust me, the comics are a lot more interesting when you have your child hanging over your shoulder listening as you read out loud from each panel, pointing to the different actions going on, laughing together.

The next step is to get your children to read to you. This will test your patience until you get used to it. Just take your time, don't jump in each time they make a mistake. When they have a question about a word or situation, ask them what they think the answer is. This will get their minds working and keep them engaged in the experience.

There have been many times when one child or another will holler out to me, "Hey, Dad, did you read 'Dilbert' today?" This begins a laughing or groaning discussion that would never have happened without the comics.

Hey, if I could sell it over the radio, surely you can try it in real life. All you have to do is grab the comics section and open it up, holding a sheet in each hand. Miraculously, a little "mini you" will suddenly appear to snuggle against your chest and listen to Daddy read the comics out loud. Any doubts you may have now will dissipate the second you hear, and feel, their laughter. Go for it.

You Read It in the Funny Papers

Here are some of the best comics to share with your kids:

"Zits" by Jerry Scott and Jim Borgman: A hilarious (and accurate!) look at life as a teenage boy.

"Blondie" by Dean Young and Denis LeBrun: You remember it from your own childhood. Follow Dagwood and Blondie's misadventures with your kids. (It might help them understand what it's like from you and your wife's perspective!)

"Pickles" by Brian Crane: This is a very clever comic featuring two senior citizens, their daughter, new son-in-law, and grandson. The situations center around how the older couple faces life through a comedic viewpoint and have prompted many discussions in our home to help my younger ones understand what they are talking about.

"LuAnn" by Greg Evans: This comic features teens and their travails coming into their own. Quite often the creators throw in some harsh reality, like a friend having cancer, and show how reactions to this serious problem vary, and that it's OK!

"Baby Blues" by Jerry Scott and Rick Kirkman: A funny look at a family as babies come into their lives and how the family dynamics change with each child. Very funny.

"Mutts" by Patrick McDonnell: This one took some getting used to. You *have* to love animals to like this one. Give it a chance and it will grow on you.

"Quigmans" by Buddy Hickerson: A one panel, wacky look at life, usually picking on a guy named Bob.

"Non Sequitur" by Wiley Miller: Another one panel comic. This guy takes on anything and everything. Very funny and very clever, and he's not afraid to take a chance.

27

You're Drivin' Me Crazy!

With four children, I've gone through the "teaching" phase for almost everything—times four. I've learned to cope with "I can't do it!" followed by screams and tears, then smiles, laughter, and finally, "What's so tough about this?" At least each learning experience felt easier than the last . . . that is, until we got to learning how to drive. Then it was my turn to scream, "I can't do it!" as my life flashed before my eyes and speeding cars zoomed right for us.

But if your child is learning to drive, or about to take her driver's license test, this is a great one-on-one activity. I decided that I would give each of my kids a driver's test before the state did, only mine would be more fun. The idea is to plan a weekend trip together in which your child acts as the driver, navigator, and trip planner. Your only job is to remain as calm as possible. The trip must take you and your child out of familiar territory. This way, your child has to study roadmaps and read highway signs. You should also make her aware that she is responsible for monitoring the fuel gauge. Be sure to include the warning that an empty fuel tank could mean miles of hiking to the next gas station—for her alone. The first time I did this with one of my children was quite a success. But that was with Son Number. 1.

First a bit about our family: We love cars. When I first met my wife-to-be, I was driving a 1964½ Mustang Pony convertible. It was a powder blue, 289 four-on-the-floor with a white top and blue and white leather interior. It was cherry. The first thing Joni said to me as I pulled up beside her was, "Nice wheels." That impressed me because she was actually talking about the car's mag wheels—not just the car itself. Our love for cars has taken us through at least twenty different vehicles during our marriage, from that Mustang to a Suburban, a Lincoln, a Jaguar XJS, a Chrysler LHS, an MGA, an Austin Healey 3000, minivans, a 1956 T-bird, and many others. When our third son was five years old, for some unknown reason he developed an obsession with Corvettes. We were visiting friends in Dallas during this obsession and actually found a dealer that had a warehouse full of old and new Corvettes. Here was this five-year-old kid running around the warehouse yelling, "Dad, Dad, come see this one!" with my other two sons and me at his heels, all salivating in kind.

So here we are, nearly ten years after our experience with our "Corvetteaholic" (who now has a Porsche 911 Turbo poster on his closet door and doesn't remember his 'vette days) and we're all still car crazy. My oldest son recently replaced the engine in his 1990 Mustang by reading a manual about how to do it. He pulled the old engine out using an A-frame hoist that he had assembled (while I was at work) on the street right in front of our house, massively ticking off everyone in the neighborhood—but that's another chapter in another book. He finished the car, and now proudly drives it to his job—as a car salesman.

I think you get the picture. But Son Number 2, also a car lover and masterful at many things, simply had trouble coordinating the skills required for driving and following directions. Because of these difficulties, he passed up the opportunity to get his license at sixteen. He waited until he was eighteen and then decided it was time. He never pushed getting out to practice driving, so neither did I. My thought was, "No practice, no license, no problem." But shortly after his eighteenth birthday, he used some money he'd saved to buy a 1966 Mustang. Then he scheduled the date and time for his written and driving tests. A car, a test date, and no experience. We had two months to pull this together. Every day, we'd hit the road after school and drive around the quieter streets of our neighborhood—which weren't too quiet once we arrived. You could hear the screech of the tires as he attempted to stop before running through stop signs and the sound of my voice pleading with him to stay in the correct lane. I know we both prayed silently as we pulled away from each intersection.

Two weeks before the driving test, he passed the written exam without a hitch. But his driving still needed work. After much prayer and consideration, I announced that he and I would be leaving on "the trip" in his Mustang on Friday morning, returning Sunday evening. According to the plan, he would drive and navigate wherever we decided to go. My only contribution would be to help out in case of an emergency . . .

and with my credit card of course. When we set off on Friday, with him at the wheel, I could feel the excitement course through him as fear ran through me. And we were off.

Initially, he asked where to turn, what direction to take, and so on, but each time I'd answer, "You tell me," forcing him to make the decision. The first time we pulled out onto the freeway, nearly becoming caught like a small rock in the groove of an eighteen-wheeler's back tires, I thought maybe this wasn't such a good idea. You must also know that I'm a great driver— I love to drive, I'd rather drive than fly—but I'm a lousy passenger. And now, here I was, trapped with a person at the wheel who could just as easily be lost in thought about his upcoming psychology paper as he could be thinking about all of those cars in the opposite lane flying toward us at high speeds.

We didn't have an accident, although we came really close a few times, and I only raised my voice and grabbed the wheel twice—oh wait, three times. But we did spend time together that we'll both talk and laugh about for the rest of our lives. At one point, as we were driving along Pacific Coast Highway, we pulled off the road at a rest area. My son got out his camera and we walked along the nature trails down toward the ocean. As he meandered along the trail shooting some of the scenic spots for his college photography class, I stood on a precipice, feeling the cool ocean breeze on my face, watching the waves break far down below. I called my wife on my cell phone to tell her where we were, what we were doing, and that we were okay. On the remainder of our journey, we'd switch off driving so he could take a break from navigating the ferociously curving coast highway or battling traffic. Along the way we con-

Drive Time

Here are some more ideas for activities to do with a driver in training:

- Go to a drive-in movie (and have the driver trainee drive, of course!).
- Set up some orange cones in a large, empty parking lot for the trainee to maneuver around. (Then set up two cones a car's length apart near the edge of the lot and have the trainee practice parallel parking.)
- Challenge your trainee to a few games of Pole Position—or whatever the hottest video driving game is nowadays.
- Watch a NASCAR or Formula One race on TV together. Or, if you and your trainee are up for it, go to the amateur drag races to see the rubber-burning action in person! (You might want to avoid the demolition derby however.)

sumed burgers, malts, candy bars, soft drinks, and biscuits and gravy at greasy spoons—the kind of joyful junk food you only get on vacation.

It was quite a road trip. We came back as two friends who had spent an adventurous weekend together. He also came back as a young man who now had confidence in his driving, and in himself. He passed his driver's test. He still asks directions and is very cautious wherever he goes, especially when friends ride with him.

Months later, my son presented me with a surprise gift to thank me for our road trip. Unbeknownst to me, he'd shot a picture of me on our stop along the ocean and presented me with a framed version. I choke up each time I look at the photo he shot of me, standing there on the edge of the world, telling my wife what a wonderful time we were having, knowing he felt that way, too.

Take a road trip with your new driver. You never know what adventures await you out there.

28

The Quest for the Holy Grail of Burgers

Granted, not every weekend plan can, or should, take up an entire weekend. The subject for this chapter is something that has been going on in my family for years. Monty Python had its search for the Holy Grail, Ponce de Leon for the fountain of youth, and Mahatma Gandhi for world peace. But as for Roberteous de Hiltonious and *familia*, our quest is for the perfect hamburger.

The beginning of my quest in our current hometown came as the result of an article in the local newspaper's food section: a list of the top ten burger joints. I decided to try them all and decide for myself which one was the best. This can work no matter where you live, presuming you like burgers. If not, then tacos, ribs, chicken—whatever. The best way to get started is to ask your children what their favorite food is. Even if it's pizza, this will work. After you choose the food, ask your neighbors, coworkers, and workers at other restaurants to rate their top ten in the food category you've chosen. That's when the fun begins.

Grab a kid; check out a spot. If you have more than one child, so much the better. You'll be able to make the rounds several times, each child compiling his list, and then compare and vote.

After you've finished your "research" you might call your local newspaper and tell them what you've done. Some of the smaller papers, the more localized the better, don't have many reporters and will often jump at the chance for a story with a cute angle. What a cool memory: a newspaper article with you and your kids in the byline.

My dad was a meat salesman for Armour and Company, so there was rarely a meal in our family that didn't include meat! Dad was "the man" for cooking two things: rib-eye steaks and burgers (see "The Best Rib Eye and Burger in the World," page 141).

I've told my children about Grandpa Harold's famous burgers many times, thus the excuse for our quest: to try to replicate this delicacy. (My daughter still thinks my burgers are the best and often begs me to open a burger place where she could be the waitress—in title only. She also announced that she'd eat the burgers and desserts and would ask the customers to pick up after themselves.)

Most of the ideas in this book focus on things to show and teach your children. This one, however, at least in my situation, is one where my kids *know* what I'm going to do (with or without them) and fight to be the one to go with me. In one city where we lived for a short time, a rather small burg, if I wasn't at home, at work, at church, or at the gym, they all knew they could find me at Dill Burger. The name sounded icky and the sign was mustard yellow and green with a picture of a pickle

The Best Rib Eye and Burger in the World

My dad cooked his rib eyes on an electric griddle with a metal bread pan turned upside-down over the steak (both of which I still have). The pan kept the juices locked in the steak—and to this day I've never found a better-tasting rib eye, though goodness knows I've looked. Dad cooked his burgers the same way, with the buns buttered and toasted on the uncovered side of the griddle.

Here's how to replicate the best burger in the world: Clump a little shredded cheddar on the meat for the last few seconds of cooking, then spread mayo on both buns and a dollop of yellow mustard (none of that Poupon stuff here!) on just one of the buns. Then layer the lettuce (chopped iceberg) and a tomato slice. The only choice of condiments we had was between dill pickles and pickle relish (my personal favorite is bread-and-butter pickles). Enjoy!

on it (which is probably why they closed a few years back), but the burgers were great.

This weekend activity is as simple as heading out for a bite at the Squeeze-In—home of the biggest, best-tasting, greasy burger you've ever let slide down your gullet—or driving a half an hour away to Sutter Creek to the Chatterbox Cafe for a fantastic gourmet, hand-formed burger on a freshly baked bun. This is one of those activities where togetherness is the main focus (aside from the burgers!). It's the perfect time for a real conversation with your child where you find out who he really is behind all of those "uh-huhs," "yeps," and "wuzzenmes."

There was a time when one of my sons and I had had one of *those* arguments. I was right and knew it, but he was, too, and knew it. There was an oppressive air of gloom over our home until my wife suggested that I take him to Geneva's. I agreed because I figured even if things didn't get better, I'd at least get a great burger out of it.

You have never seen a more awful looking place than Geneva's. It's about one-quarter the size of a Dairy Queen and sits on a main street, on a corner, in a bad part of town. Were it not for the long line of tattered to tailored folks standing in front of what could be a bookie's window, you'd pass by thinking the business had been shut down by the city years ago. But, my-oh-my, the burgers that come out of this dump! A buttered, grilled, sesame seed bun with mayo on both pieces and a dollop of yellow mustard on one side, quality beef, shredded lettuce, delicious tomatoes, and dill pickles. Plus free refills on drinks.

In silence we drove, two men from two different generations, both feeling in the right and wronged (and only one of them paying, of course). We arrived, we waited, we ordered, we sat . . . in silence. Our burgers came, with large, well-salted fries in a separate little paper bag, and we began to eat. And talk. And apologize. And forgive. Both of us. Thanks, Dad.

29

Was I Hustled (Or Was I the Hustler)?

Is there a dad among you who hasn't cracked the cue ball at the racked fifteen down the table praying for the eight to drop on the break? I did it once, and I'm not the greatest pool player. This is an activity that kids can enjoy at any age, even if they can barely reach over the rail to push one ball toward another. If your children are old enough to hold a cue stick and tall enough to use it with some degree of authority, take 'em to the pool hall—more than likely listed as a "family billiards parlor" nowadays. Like other smoky places with bad reps of the past, most pool halls today barely resemble the places your parents warned you about. Families are now encouraged at most of them. They're smoke-free and well lighted inside and out. I think they finally figured out that to survive, they had to cater to the family business. (Though, as a precaution, I recommend that you check out the place before you just assume it's family friendly.)

Not a pool shark? On the Web, type *billiards* into your favorite search engine and you'll find enough information to make even the most rank amateur at least sound like a pro. You can learn about eight ball, nine ball, the actual game of billiards, and on and on. Kids today claim that video games help them with hand–eye coordination. Let them try pool. Not only does it help develop better hand–eye coordination, but they can also learn to hit the cue ball with just the right "English" to dazzle and amaze their friends—and themselves—with amazing trick shots that video games cannot touch. (Just so you don't have to look it up, English in this sense means "spin around the vertical axis deliberately imparted to a ball that is driven or rolled." Thanks, *Merriam Webster's Collegiate Dictionary!*)

In an earlier chapter, I said "weekend moments" could come up at any time, and that you should take advantage of them when they do. One came up for my son and me on a recent Monday night. I had been sitting on the edge of my daughter's bed, scratching her head and telling her goodnight while my wife was getting ready for bed. I couldn't wait to get to bed myself. I was exhausted and for the last two hours had stumbled around the house in a daze. We had just come off daylight saving time, and so the pitch of night came an hour earlier, lulling me with its song of sleep. As I sat there, I heard the sound of footsteps approaching. It was my oldest son, dressed, not for bed, but for going out. I made the big mistake of asking where he was heading.

"Oh, I was just going to tell you and Mom goodnight. I'm going out to shoot pool."

Never one to miss a moment where I can put my foot as far as possible down my throat, and, in this case, to the bottom of my stomach, I said, "Well, sometime when you think you're brave enough, you might want to challenge your old man to a game. I've been known to run a few tables in my lifetime."

Gauntlet laid, gauntlet seized, to my ultimate dismay.

"What's wrong with tonight?" He smiled, knowing that I was dragging my tail lower than a mule on a labor strike.

"Who are you going with?" I asked, hoping that his answer would guarantee that there would be a crowd of his friends going with him and that there wouldn't really be a spot for dear old Dad.

"No one," he replied—and I thought I detected a slight hint of sadness at his admission.

Boy, did my mind sit up and start slapping my brain cells around. I realized rather quickly how throughout this book I continually reinforce the importance of seizing a moment when it comes. And here was a moment staring me right in my sleepy face.

As I stood up, trying not to appear as old as I now felt, I said, "Hold on, I'll see if Mom can get the other kids to sleep, and if so I'll go with you and just give you a little example of why they called your dad 'Rack 'Em Up Robert' back in college."

My son, being the bright kid that he is, quickly replied, "Dad, it's always the loser who racks, not the winner."

But I decided to go anyway. As we walked outside, he headed straight to *his* car, a first. When we go anyplace together, I always drive because 1) I like to drive, and 2) we can burn my car's gas, not his. So I knew this night was going to be different somehow. It occurred to me as I strapped on my seatbelt that I had never ridden in his car before. When I said so, he agreed, which I took to mean that he'd been waiting for me

Pool Sharks

Here are the rules to the two most popular variations of pool:

Eight ball: The goal is to clear the table of all your balls (solids or stripes), leaving the black eight ball on the table until the end. Once you've cleared your balls, you must call the pocket into which you plan to shoot the eight—even if up to now you've been playing slop. If the eight ball "scratches" (goes into any pocket other than the one called), you lose. If the cue ball goes into *any* pocket, you lose.

Nine ball: Unlike eight ball, where you must eliminate either the stripes or the solids before attacking the eight ball, you can go after the nine right away. However, you must do so with a combination if there are balls on the table other than the nine. This means you can shoot at (and hit) the next ball in the rotation, knocking it into the nine. If the nine goes in, you win. Now, you can make the game more restrictive if you choose, say, having to call each shot, eliminating the lucky-shot factor.

The point is to have fun, not get so competitive that the joy of being together disappears. If you have to win to feel good, you shouldn't play. You'll lose your child fast by trouncing them for your own selfish reasons. Teach them sportsmanship. Teach them how to win *and lose* graciously.

By the way, a game of pool can be anything with any rules you and your child decide upon. The younger the child, the less restrictive the rules. Be flexible—it is, after all, just a game.

to do so. He had completely rebuilt the engine in this car and was quite proud of that fact. Telling him that I was also proud wasn't enough; this is what he had wanted.

On the way to the pool parlor he told me about his car, how the compression was off, how the alternator was set too low (he demonstrated how the panel lights got brighter as he put the pedal to the metal). I, in turn, pointed out the various police and/or sheriff's vehicles in the vicinity.

When we arrived at a billiards parlor I'd never been to before (but which apparently my son had), we walked through the doors into a huge billiard emporium blaring music and packed with people of all ages, more of them my son's age than mine.

The young man at the reservations desk greeted my son by his driver's license name, not his nickname. My son exchanged his ID for a rack of balls, led me to a quieter section of the building, and proceeded to set up the table for a game.

"Eight ball?" he asked.

"You bet," I replied as I selected a cue from the rack in the corner and then proceeded to roll the stick across the felt of the adjoining table, acting as if I knew what I was doing.

For the next two-and-a-half hours, we played eight ball, nine ball, rotation, oddball nine ball, scratch-and-you-spot-your-highest-pointer, and even tried a few trick shots some of his friends had shown him. At one point he said he'd be right back, so I naturally assumed he was going to the bathroom. In a few moments he returned with a pitcher of root beer and two Styrofoam cups for us to share. You have no idea what an incredible moment that was. He was treating me like a friend, not just his dad. We cheered for each other, booed one another, laughed, and even slapped hands on a few really cool (and really lucky) shots.

We decided on one last game: eight ball . . . and the loser pays for the evening. It seemed that he had spent most of the night blocking my every shot, forcing me to bank here or curve the cue ball there. Now, however, he was starting to get hot, making a run on the five, the eleven, a lucky three banker on the one. But then he made the fatal mistake of rolling the eight ball into the side pocket rather than the usually unlucky number thirteen. I couldn't let him lose like that and ruin our evening, so even though we hadn't played with this rule the rest of the evening, I suggested we spot the eight, meaning it was still anyone's game. I made a run and missed. He sank one then missed. Then I cleared the board, ending with perfect position on the eight ball, which clung precariously close to the edge of the corner pocket. Should I pull a Tom Cruise from *The Color of Money* and miss on purpose while looking as if I'm trying to make it? I wondered. And if I did, would he be as angry as Paul Newman got, quit the game, and then make me walk home? (You have to watch that movie! See chapter 3, "Off to the Movies" for more.) Or should I play the ball as I would want him to play it against me, giving it my best shot? I won't tell you which I did because one way is noble; the other is just admitting that I'm a lousy shot. He won, I paid, and we both left admitting we'd had a great time.

On the ride home, amid the camaraderie, I realized I hadn't felt tired the entire evening. As we walked through the front door at home, we shook hands and thanked each other for a great time. As he turned to head off to his room I nearly called him back to say, "Let's not end it yet—let's go get a burger!" But the moment passed, and I heard him on the phone with a friend. I yawned and turned toward my bedroom when I clearly overheard: "Yeah, with my dad." And then a laugh. "It was pretty cool."

Pretty cool? Nah . . . the impromptu night at the pool hall with my son was *very, very,* cool.

30

Get Your Head in the Game

If you have more than one child, some weekends you'll want to plan an activity that includes them all, for your sake as well as theirs. Siblings need time together where they can compete against each other, or sometimes team together, without their friends around. Friends often make siblings feel as though they can't be affectionate toward one another without spawning put-downs or looking dorky.

One way we've overcome this in our family is to play board games together—even inventing our own if the mood strikes us. Our game cupboard is overflowing with Scrabble, Monopoly, Balderdash, Boggle, Yahtzee, Braintrust, Trivial Pursuit, Win Lose or Draw, and on and on. We also love dominoes, tri-ominos, and card games. I grew up with parents who loved a card game called Rook. I learned the game and taught it to my wife so that we could play it with relatives at a family reunion. My mother was (and still is) a great Rook player; she even has a group of regulars who play daily at the assisted-living facility where she now resides.

The point of telling you about Rook is that a few years back, my mom was diagnosed with a brain tumor. She had already lost many of her physical and mental faculties, and at her advanced age, surgery was risky. But her doctor, a family friend, told my brother, Ken, that as bad as the operation sounded, without it, her chances of retaining any quality of life were minimal. She had the operation (the tumor was the size of a grapefruit) and for a while we weren't sure if she would recover. But she pulled through. It took nearly two years for her to fully recover, but now she's back, stronger and feistier than ever and once again, kicking butt at Rook. She and her ninety-two-year-old partner just won a Rook tournament at her place.

Mom surprised us a few months ago with an impromptu visit. She flew El Cheapo Airlines with about seventy stops between Mississippi and California, but she made it. As a surprise for Nana, we had taught the kids to play Rook, giving us a lot of family time together in preparation for her visit. When she arrived, we announced that there would be a Rook tournament during her visit. We just had one problem: Everyone wanted to be on Nana's team. So all the kids got their chance to be Nana's partner, and they knew they were pretty much guaranteed a win. Nana did what she came out here to do: create wonderful memories for her grandchildren—and show us that she's still as formidable a force as ever when it comes to Rook. If they ever make an infomercial for that game, eighty-five-year-young Jessie Lea "Nana" Hilton should be the spokesperson. She's still got the touch.

As far as creating your own games, it's not as big a job as you might fear. I'll give you two examples.

Necessary Board Games

- Guesstures
- Win Lose or Draw
- Taboo
- Tri-ominoes
- Uno
- Pictionary
- Trivial Pursuit
- Scrabble
- Cash Flow (twenty times better than Monopoly)
- Yahtzee
- Risk
- Rummikub

My bride, the lovely and talented Joni, is an incredibly gifted woman. She is the author of many books on subjects including humor, how-tos, and even a guide called *Family Fun Book*, in which she offers a cornucopia of ideas that could become games. In this book, for example, she gives several ideas for turning math into games, and using that as your template, you could make lots of different school subjects into games.

We did this when we were having trouble teaching one of our children the alphabet. We purchased a huge section of cardboard and began to lay out a life-size game where each time you answered a question dealing with the alphabet, you got to move ahead a few spaces, depending on the number value given to that particular question. Our son got very involved in the game, which allowed him to move like a giant chess piece across the room, sometimes running, other times hopping, most times laughing, and as we had hoped, all the while learning. To this day, that child, who is now in college, can still remember his alphabet. Am I a great teacher, or what?

Second, remember that games you create can be based on anything: school, sports, other games, or nothing at all. I'll prove it.

To test my theory, I sat the kids down at our dining table the other night and told them we were going to create a game expressly for this book. After the usual protests you expect from kids who think they're actually going to have to work at something, I told them the rules for this game are simple: There are no rules. They can choose how and what the game will be, and it didn't have to match up with the previous player's contributions. We took turns around the table, each kid giving his or her part of the game. The point of this exercise was to prove that we could have fun together making up a silly, nonsensical game—even if we didn't actually *play* the game. What follows is as close to an actual transcript of our game-creation round table as I can provide. (I was writing longhand and hope I can interpret my chicken scratches correctly, as I'm sure you'll want to get the home version and play it with your family immediately.)

Let's call the game Bamboozle after a TV pilot that I made for ABC television. The show was fun, the network loved it, but it just never worked—and this won't either. Here goes:

"It's a board game that everybody has to dress up to play."

"I quit. No, wait, you have to dress up in a laser-force T-shirt."

"You *have* to be wearing any color you want."

"What happens if we're wearing a color someone else made you put on?"

"Then you're out of the game."

"The board has to be thirty-three feet in diameter—no, no, it has three bases thirty-three meters apart and in the middle there's a mound. But it all has to be on the board."

"It has squares you move to, like Candyland."

"Uh, uh, trying to think of stuff, like Calvin Ball, but there's no rules, I know."

"You have to capture a flag somehow."

"It's kinda like you can go to the fair on the board and they have animals and you can adopt them and stuff."

"You can only spend half of the game on the ground, stay on the ground for the count of one, and in the air for the count of two and three."

"I'm totally confused. But I get a head start."

"Every time you pass Go you collect two hundred dollars."

"If you have less than five dollars you have to dress up like a hobo and you also get to go to concerts and they're all 'N Sync."

"Hey, it's a *board* game. When you fold it up, don't all the animals die?"

"Only I can pass Go, and I always win."

"Plastic poop for all the animals. The object of the game is to *not* have to clean up after the animals. You land on a certain square, you can give your poop to someone else."

"You have to shoot down the other players with a jet plane that was hijacked from the airstrip in the outfield."

"There's a Ricky Martin; he wears gold bellbottoms and there's a model salon and you get to go to the pumpkin patch and field trips around the world."

(Big pause here.)

"I'm done."

"I'm done."

"I'm done."

"Wait, wait, wait. All the pop stars come to your house, even Mary Kate and Ashley."

"No, wait, here's what really happens: You play the gopher game, but replace the gophers with pop stars who she had come over to the house, and whack them in the head with mallets . . . and the game ends."

And it did.

31

You Can Hear a Pin Drop!

Bowling! In a word, the quickest, easiest, and most fun way to initiate some time alone with your child. This activity works with practically any age group, as long as your child can pick up a ball and throw it in the general direction of the pins.

The first time I ventured into a bowling alley, I was with my older brother and one of his pals. The fact that I, the younger brother, was allowed to been seen in public with them was in itself a minor miracle, but to take me with them to this smoky, poorly lit, loud, manly-man kind of place was, to me, simply awesome. This was in the late fifties and the bowling alley was very old, only twelve lanes wide. There were guys whose job it was to hover over the pins and, as they were knocked down, reset them for the next bowler. I remember that the bowling balls were chipped and ugly, and I couldn't figure out how to keep the ball from heading into the gutters on either side of the lane.

A few years later, there was a grand opening for a new bowling alley in town, built close to the new Piggly-Wiggly.

Wow, had things changed! I walked in to a thirty-six-lane, brightly lit, kid-friendly environment that served great grilled cheese sandwiches and malts. Kids packed the place, and I didn't see a beer bottle or a cigarette anywhere. And I already knew how to make the ball go quickly into the gutters.

At the time, the bowling-alley business was trying to revitalize itself, cleaning up its image and going after a younger customer base. Of course, there was nothing to be done about the fact that, unless you were extremely talented—like Butch LeBlanc, who threw strike after strike (turns out his dad had owned the old bowling alley where Butch had worked setting pins and practicing after hours)—you spent a lot of time watching ball after ball swiftly drop off to the side as the automatic pinsetters lifted load after load of untouched, unscathed, sparkling new pins. How could they overcome this bad public relations?

If you haven't been bowling in a few years, you're in for a surprise. The greatest invention for making bowling interesting and keeping bowlers interested is, in my humble opinion, bumpers. These are round, rubber tubes placed in the gutters to prevent the ball from dropping in, keeping it in play, assuring the novice bowler that he'll knock down at least the seven or the ten pin—and usually a few more than that. It's great to watch a kid howl with delight as he waddles up to the foul line (and many times quite a bit beyond it), bends over, and shoves his light-as-a-feather ball toward the pins, wide eyes staring as the ball rolls excruciatingly slowly (for the dad) down the apparently mile-long alley, bruising the bumper then grudgingly heading back into the line of fire to do battle with the pins, dropping a few in the process. Priceless!

If your child is too old or too big to use the bumpers, bowling is still a lot of fun. The lanes have become user-friendly with another device that helps take the worry out of looking dumb: Quick—what's a turkey, how do you add your score if you had a spare followed by an open frame, and what happens in the tenth frame if one of you gets a strike? Not to worry! It's all automated, so scoring a game is no longer the nightmare it once was.

Getting past my rough start in bowling, over the years I became quite proficient at the sport, even managing a bowling alley for a brief time after my tour of duty with the Navy. I wasn't the greatest manager, but I did get to bowl a bunch of games every day for free. Once, home for a visit, I invited my dad to go bowling with me, something I had never been able to get him to do. To my surprise and pleasure, he said yes. He'd never been in a bowling alley in his life, so I, the *professional*, gave him much more information than he could possibly use about how to select a ball (he just grabbed the first one he came to) and the proper shoes (he kept his street shoes on), and, of course, the correct way to throw the ball (which he must have watched me demonstrate with total amusement). I began by showing him how to wipe your hands on your personal bowling towel (didn't everybody have one?) or how to use the blower on the ball return to make sure your "delivery hand" was dry. I demonstrated how to lift the ball with both hands, cupping it with your left hand underneath while gently inserting your right hand into the holes, making sure your fingers "feel" the ball. Next, I showed him the proper way to use the four-, five-, and six-step approach, and of course,

First-Time Bowlers, Take Note

Here are a few tips for your first bowling outing:

Wear clothes that feel loose and comfortable. If you're taking a daughter, have her wear pants, as bending over to throw the ball can be a little too revealing, plus, some people are known to slip and fall on their backsides as they become a bit more, um, relaxed in their game.

Select a ball that's a little lighter than you might expect to use; you'll soon discover that it tends to become heavier as the game progresses. To make sure you get the right fit, try out as many balls as you have patience for. Place the two middle fingers of your throwing hand into the ball. They should fit easily up to the second knuckle. Your thumb should fit all the way to the base of your hand. With your fingers in the ball, attempt to lift your thumb out while keeping your middle fingers in. If your thumb won't release easily, or it releases with a pop, that ball is not for you. Take your time and find the right ball for both you and your child. You can even try a few different balls during the game. A ball that fits poorly can cause blisters. If the ball is too big, it can be very embarrassing when it flies off backward straight at the spectators behind you. A too-small ball may not release from your hand when it's supposed to, popping off a second or two after its intended release, arching high and then dropping like a cannonball onto the wooden alleyway with a loud and embarrassing crack. (Not that I've ever experienced either of these situations.)

how to lift your hand in the "handshake" position when releasing the ball toward the second arrow, giving your ball just the right trajectory so it curves between the one and three pins, assuring a high count of downed pins, if not a strike.

My dad just sat there smiling, the kind, patient man that he was. I told him he could go first and so he did. Dad walked on to the ready deck, picked up the ball with his right hand (heresy!), and in one motion turned, walked to the foul line, tossed the ball, and without looking, turned back toward me, retreated to his chair and sat down. I watched in amazement as the ball plundered its way down the lane, dead on toward the head pin, smashing into and totally annihilating the pins. *STRIKE!*

I took my turn in somewhat of a daze. To this day, I still don't remember what I rolled. What I do remember, clear as a bell, was the subsequent conversation:

"Your turn, Dad."

"Why do I need to throw another one?"

"It's your turn."

With a wizened smile beginning to break on his face, he continued, "Son, isn't the object of the game to knock down all of those wooden things down there at the end?"

"Yes, Sir."

"Well, didn't I just do that?"

"Yes, Sir."

"And if I threw another ball and did less than that, I'd just be going down in my score, right?"

"Yes, Sir."

"Then I think I'll just quit while I still have a perfect score."

And he did.

Give your kids a memory . . . take them bowling.

32

Now, Class, Pay Attention

A fun and easy weekend idea is to take a class with your child. There are lots of subjects you'll both enjoy—from crafts to academic subjects to auto shop (for a list of more ideas, see "Back to School," page 163). You could even go to one of those giant home-improvement stores and take a class there. Give a child who's heading off to college a gift of a tool set, then take a class together to learn the proper use for each tool. Or start with more challenging topics like how to change an electrical socket or how to properly use cutting tools so that the wood—not your precious digits—gets sawed off safely.

How about a class in auto mechanics? Thanks to such a class, my son, the new driver, successfully changed the oil in his car, and then saved even more money by changing the belts on his engine. This is great stuff to share on a weekend.

I once signed up for a class with my daughter at one of those do-it-yourself ceramics places in the mall. When we entered the place, there must have been a hundred other little girls like mine (but not as cute) with their mommies, all chattering and chirping about this and that piece of ceramic. I asked my daughter if she wanted to come back another day when Mom could be with her, but she said no, insisting that having her dad here was great (would that Dad felt the same!).

What you do is pick out the piece of ceramic you want to paint, select all of the paints and designs you want to decorate your choice with, and have at it. We paid about $5 for the heart box my daughter selected and another $2.50 for the firing and glazing. This process means two trips out together: one to choose and paint, another to pick up your piece after it's fired, glazed, and dried (which takes about twelve hours).

Despite the fact that I was the only dad in the place, my daughter and I had fun doing this project together. I selected a mug, which I painted in a seventies retro style. She was protective of her artwork, showing me her work on the outside of the heart-shaped box, but not what she had painted on the inside. After the class (which is less about listening to someone talk as it is about learning by doing), we had lunch, window-shopped, and went for an ice cream treat. It was about five hours of uninterrupted Dad–daughter time. It was great.

I went back on Monday without her to pick up our crafts so that I could present hers when I picked her up at school. On the way home from school, she kept inspecting her heart box and giggling, but not sharing with me what she had painted on the inside of her brightly decorated treasure.

When we got home, she ran to her mom's supply room where we keep the wrapping paper and shut the door. Moments later she emerged and presented me with a hastily

Back to School

But this time, you choose the class to take—and don't forget to have fun. Here's a short list of some classes you might consider taking with your child:

- Cartooning
- Genealogy
- Pottery
- Magic
- Sewing
- Dog training/obedience school
- Cooking
- Foreign language
- Religion
- Swimming
- Golf
- Martial arts
- Archery
- Fencing
- Sign language
- Ballroom dance

wrapped gift—exactly the size of the heart box she'd been working on. As I unwrapped it, wondering aloud what was inside, she stood there beaming. I opened the present to find it was the heart box she had painted with bright colors that Saturday.

I kissed her and thanked her, but she pulled away, insisting that I look inside the box. When I lifted the lid, I saw what she had been keeping from me. Inside, she had painted another heart, with the word "I" above it and the word "DADDY" below it.

Some weekend activities with your children may take you out of your comfort zone, but the rewards are well worth it.

33

Permission to Come Aboard, Sir!

No matter where you live, it's likely there's a military facility within driving distance for a weekend jaunt. I'm proud to be an American and to have served in the Navy, but regardless, it's a great way to spend time with your children and teach them a bit about our country's armed forces. Heightened security might make visiting a base tougher, but it makes the experience all the more real.

I served aboard the U.S.S. *Randolph*, an aircraft carrier that, like many of our nation's military ships, has an incredible history. The *Randolph* was commissioned in 1943 and sent to Iwo Jima to support U.S. servicemen in that battle. While at anchor, a suicide bomber hit the ship, killing twenty-five sailors and injuring more than a hundred others. More recently, the *Randolph* was picked to be the main recovery ship for John Glenn's moon orbit flight in 1962 and was used later during the Cuban missile crisis, helping with the blockade. A victim of budget cuts, the *Randolph* met its untimely end in 1975 when it was sold off for scrap.

My children have heard many stories about my adventures as a young man aboard this floating city of nearly 4,000 men and between eighty and a hundred aircraft. In one, I told the story of the time I served as a photographer on the flight deck filming landings using a handheld, 16 mm, black-and-white camera (prevideo, of course), as was my assignment. Each time we had flight ops, my job was to shoot footage of each plane as it lowered its tail hooks in anticipation of dropping down to the flight deck, where the hook was supposed to grab one of three cables that helped stop the rapidly descending rocket. If the pilot failed to snag one of the cables, he would quickly power up again to avoid running off the angled flight deck and plunging into the ocean. The life-and-death decision had to be made in a split second.

I always stood in the exact same spot for this assignment, leaning against a stack of lifeboats for comfort, but this particular day, a voice warned me three distinct times to move from that spot. I ignored the voice the first two times, but the third time, I reluctantly moved. No sooner had I moved than one of the jets came in, tail hook down, and missed all but the last cable. Thinking he had missed them all, the pilot attempted to lift off—until he felt the drag of the cable and shut off his power again. The nose of the jet had lifted, but when the pilot killed the power, the plane slammed down onto the flight deck with such force that the front wheel housing shattered, sending shrapnel across the deck—right into the pile of lifeboats where I normally stood. I'm a much better listener to my inner voice now and have always hoped that sharing this story with my children would help them trust their own instincts.

It was an interesting twist of fate when one of my sons had the opportunity to go with his Scout troop on an overnighter aboard the U.S.S. *Hornet* at its permanent berth as a Navy museum in Alameda, California. Not enough dads had signed up as chaperones for the outing, so my son asked me if I could fill in. If you've never spent the night camping out with Scouts, it is indeed an experience you must try—at least once.

When we arrived at the pier, I felt like I had returned to Norfolk, Virginia, where I had been stationed as a young sailor. The *Hornet* was an exact replica of the *Randolph*, which were both in the CVS classification. As we approached the gangplank to board the carrier, I began to have a really weird feeling. The minute I entered the hangar deck, the smells of diesel fuel and paint permeated my senses completely, taking me back in time. My son put his hand on my shoulder, realizing I was lost in reverie, and became the father for the moment, helping direct me along as I reverted back thirty years. I never realized how deeply being in the Navy had entered my subconscious mind. I spent that night and the next day sharing stories and touring this *Randolph* replica, showing my son the cramped, four-high bunks my buddies and I had slept in, the metal, orange-crate-size lockers that held all of our possessions. I even located the photo lab, a facility much smaller than the one I remembered working in. As I showed my son around, we bumped into the chief engineer of the *Hornet* museum. I explained our expedition and that I had served on the *Randolph*, and he led us on an off-limits tour, ending in a section of the ship that wasn't yet open to the public. It was a section of the ship dedicated to photos and other memorabilia of the

Share Your Personal History

Visiting military installations will give your children a glimpse into history, as well as the present day. But any trips you take with your children to spots from your own childhood or young adulthood are a great way to spend time together. It's a way to walk with them through some of the windows of your life before you became "Dad." All the while, tell or retell stories about your childhood. Being on the actual spots where the stories took place will make it that much more special.

Here are some ideas for places to go:

Your elementary, middle, or high school—or even your college campus. Show them the fields you played sports on, the science lab where your chemistry project blew a hole in the wall, or the stage where you performed with your school rock band.

The site of your first job. The Dairy Queen that's *still* there after all these years, Big Al's Auto Body, or maybe your family's farm or business.

The place you met their mom. Tell them exactly how you felt the first time you saw her, how the two of you met, and what made it special. The location doesn't matter—but being there with your child will really bring it to life. (Of course, if you and your wife met in a bar or other place unsuitable for kids, you might want to rethink this one!)

Site of another important event in your life. Your kids might never have heard of Woodstock (and maybe *you* were too young to go), but if you attended an event like that as a young person, your kids will enjoy visiting the site and hearing your stories.

U.S.S. *Randolph*. My son and I spent the next few hours, he in rapt attention, as I shared a part of my past with him.

We later walked the entire ship, from the forecastle (pronounced FOLKS-ul) to the fantail, as I told him stories about storms that sent waves crashing over the bow of the huge ship, and about an explosion at sea that ripped off the starboard elevator, killing several men and destroying one jet. We walked the flight deck and sat down by one of the catapults, staring at the full moon across the bay, shining brightly on that cloudless night.

Reverently, my son asked me to show him the spot where I had nearly lost my life the day the jet crashed its front-wheel assembly. Before that moment I had chosen not to recall that incident during our visit. As we went aft to the spot so vividly etched in my memory, I felt my son make the connection between the story I had told and the actual spot on the ship. Touching the now-empty metal cage that had housed the lifeboats made my experience come to life—for him and for me.

We asked another Scout to snap pictures of my son and me at that spot and elsewhere around the ship. I'm glad I listened to that little voice that told me to move out of the way—and the one that told me to go with my son on that trip.

34

Going, Going, Gone!

How can you write a book about weekend activities to do with your children and not include taking them to a ball game? It doesn't matter if it's major league, minor league, high school—or even T-ball. Spending time together in the bleachers with a hot dog and a root beer—it just doesn't get much better than that. If your child is interested, sign him or her up for T-ball or little league. Maybe even volunteer to help coach. (Just *don't* be one of those jerk dads who yells at the umpires or the head coaches. They are just dads like you trying their best to help out. And you'll embarrass your child, too, which could make him not want you around or might even make him quit the team in frustration.) I believe in the adage "Sports don't *build* character, they *reveal* character." Teach your children about sportsmanship and team play. Spend time playing catch and shagging fly balls. Offer advice when they ask for it. Rent instructional videos to show them how the pros do it. Rent *The Natural* or *The Rookie*. This is a weekend activity that can become a lifetime activity.

A buddy of mine from high school, Wayne Smith, called me the other day. We've stayed in touch through the years. I told him that I was working on this book and asked him if he had a story about a special time with his son. He chuckled and said, yes, indeed, he had chronicled one such special memory in his journal. When I heard it, I asked if I could include it in these pages. In my pal Wayne's own words, here is a story of one boy, his dad, and a ball game:

"It was in 1989 when I told my seven-year-old son Jordan that we were going to go see a baseball game at the Astrodome in Houston. He excitedly began telling me and everyone else he saw that he was going to catch a ball at the game. As a parent, the last thing you want to do is watch your child build his hopes on some highly improbable thing happening, a dream that will only cause disappointment if it doesn't come true.

"The initial purpose for the trip to Houston was to get a final checkup and release from the doctor who had recently operated on my wrist. I thought it would be a great time to take Jordan to see the Astrodome and a chance to watch his favorite baseball team, the Astros, play. I was looking forward to taking him there; it's one of those daddy things we love to do.

"When he said he was going to take his glove with him so that he could catch a ball, my heart sank, knowing that the chances of a little guy like him catching a foul ball or home run in the Astrodome were slim, at best. I didn't want him to get his hopes up, but the more I warned him about the other 40,000-plus baseball fans with similar plans of catching a ball, and the fact that there were very few balls hit to the hinterlands where our seats were located, the more resolved he was to 'catch a ball.'

"From our home in Lake Charles, Louisiana, it was a two-hour trip to Houston, the doctor's office, and the game. He continued to tell everyone he saw, 'I'm going to the Astrodome with my Daddy. I'm gonna catch a ball.' He told his grandmothers, the neighbors, he even told the postman. And every time he told someone, my heart would break because I knew it wasn't going to happen. But he never let up. When we were finally in the car, ready to go, Jordan sat there, smiling, staring straight ahead, his glove on his hand. He was ready.

"When we arrived at the medical office for my examination, he began his speech again. He told the doctor, the nurse, the man who had made my cast—in fact, anyone who would listen. When we left to go grab a bite before the game, he resumed his patter with our waitress at the Hard Rock Café. She winked at me and mouthed, 'Cute kid.'

"As we were getting out of the car in the Astrodome parking lot, I discreetly tossed his glove to the rear corner of the back seat, knowing that he wouldn't need it and that I'd end up having to carry that glove around all night if it came with us. Of course, he caught me. He gave me an exasperated look and said, 'Daddy, give me my glove. I am gonna catch a ball.'

"We did the tourist thing, visited the gift shop and bought a poster of Mike Scott, one of the Astros' premier pitchers, plus an Astros pennant. I was now carrying the poster, the pennant, peanuts, a Coke, and Jordan's glove. That is also a daddy thing.

"Sometime around the sixth inning, we moved down from our cheap, faraway, right-field seats to some much nicer

To the Ball Game

Going to a professional sports game is very exciting. But, hitting the minor leagues is a real blast. These teams actually compete to make the fans happy. They have various events and contests for adults and children. College games are exciting also. You get a chance to see players compete for the thrill of playing, *not* the thrill of being payed.

One other tip: If you get the chance to sing "Take Me Out to the Ball Game," here's a wacky way to do it. I learned this from a barbershop quartet.

Rather than starting off the normal way, link the first two words together so that the song begins "Takeme"— as one word. This throws the entire beat of the song off, leaving you with a surprise ending. Here's how the lyrics should go now:

Takeme out to the ball game, take
Me out to the crowd. Buy
Me some peanuts and Cracker Jacks. I
Don't care if I never get back, for
It's root, root, root for the home team. If
Theydon't win it's a shame, for
It's *one,two,* three strikes you're out at the
Old ball game — (extra beat here where the song should have ended)

End the song with your arms outstretched for a big finish—looking puzzled over the missing ending.

ones about fourteen rows from field level between third base and left field, hoping no one would come along and bump us from our newly poached seats. As we settled in, the people sitting around us saw the smiling seven-year-old with his glove and they smiled back. I just sort of shrugged my shoulders with that 'Daddy-gave-in' look on my face. They understood.

"After concentrating on the game for a few minutes, Jordan took off his glove and handed it to me, his attention now on his bag of peanuts.

"Terry Puhl, the Astros' right fielder came up to bat. The count was one strike and three balls. On the next pitch, a fastball down and inside, Puhl swung for the fence, but fouled it off instead. Jordan continued cracking peanut shells as the ball arched toward us and bounced off the back of a seat about thirty feet away. Then all the angels in heaven made it bounce through the air and land right in Jordan's lap. The ball fell out of his lap and hit the floor. With peanuts flying through the air, he scrambled down between the seats, searching for the ball along with about six other desperate pairs of hands. After a moment of breathless prayer by me, up popped a kid with the biggest grin I've ever seen, and then a fist shot skyward as Jordan raised the baseball high above his head in triumph. When the celebration of his catch died down, he calmly turned to me, looked me straight in the eye, and said, 'See, I told you so.'

"So many emotions rushed through me at that moment. I knew that this would be one of those memories that Jordan and I would treasure forever. His telling everyone that he was going to 'catch a ball,' and then holding that ball majestically aloft when he did taught me a very valuable lesson: I learned never to dismiss my child's dreams, no matter what the odds.

"At the time I write this, Jordan has become a fine young man. Among his achievements, he has been a batboy and bullpen catcher for the Shreveport Captains baseball team, the AA farm team for the San Francisco Giants. Once, when Jordan was five years old, he told me that when he grew up he was going to be a professional baseball player. Who I am to say differently?"

35

One for the Record Books

In 1979, I was the emcee for a TV game show pilot called "The Guinness Game" based on the bestselling book series, *Guinness World Records*. In the time between making the pilot and selling the show into syndication, I had already moved on to host a different show (which was unfortunately less successful than the world record show). Later, the Guinness world record theme came back to TV in a series known as "Guinness World Records: Primetime."

Guinness World Records got started back in 1951, when a man by the name of Sir Hugh Beaver, who was managing director of Guinness Brewery, went on a "shooting party" (the English phrase for "hunting trip"). As the Guinness Web site tells it, he and another hunter got into an argument over what was the fastest game bird in Europe, the golden plover or the grouse. (Do you know the answer? I'll give it to you at the end of this chapter.) It was then that Sir Hugh realized that a book full of such information would be a great way to promote his beer. The first book of records came out in 1955 and went to the top of the bestsellers' list in the United Kingdom by Christmas of that year.

So, although Guinness world records may not make lasting TV show fodder, it might be a lot of fun for you and your children to try to get in the book by setting or bettering a current record.

Here's how to get started:

First, decide what you want to do—challenge an existing record or go for an entirely new one. There are several ways to check out current records. Every year, a new edition of the Guinness record book comes out, first in a rather pricey hardback edition, then, later in the year, in less-expensive paperback. There is also a Web site: www.guinnessrecords.com.

The index of the paperback edition I have lists more than 400 categories (yes, that's *categories*, not individual records)—everything from parachute escapes to hula-hoop spins to body piercings (probably not the record you want to challenge *your* kids with!). For a sample of some of the wackier records, see "You Did What—with How Many People?" on page 179.

The point is to pick whatever activity you think you and your kids can make or break a record for, follow the rules, and see what happens. If you succeed, you and your children will receive an official certificate acknowledging that you have set or broken a world record. Pretty neat, eh?

Two of my children and I have decided to go for our own world record. After much consideration, we chose to document our search for the largest number of folded (doubled up) potato chips in a large bag (20 ounces) of Lay's potato chips.

When creating a new type of record, the rules require a "challenge that is interesting, requires skill, is safe, and . . . is likely to attract challenges from other people." Hmmm. Ours is safe, I think it's interesting, and I'm sure others will challenge. The "requires skill" part is open to question.

Documentation is a must. Having been in the TV news business for many years, I know that on slow news days, you're more likely to see coverage of "record-breaking" events, though I'm just not sure ours would make the cut even on the slowest of slow news days. My best advice is to videotape your efforts at home. If the event you and your child choose must be timed, make sure a clock is visible onscreen at all times. You also need at least two independent witnesses, that is, someone not related to you. The witnesses must confirm that they have seen the record-setting attempt as well as its completion, and that you followed the specified guidelines at all times. (You'll need to contact Guinness World Records to ascertain the specific guidelines for your event. You can send e-mail to infouk@guinness records.com.)

Even if your attempt to set a record never makes it into the book, the real fun comes from planning and trying the event together. I know our attempt will never get in the book because we eat the double-folded potato chips as fast as we find them. Once I revealed to my kids that the double-folded chips were my favorite, the real challenge became getting to them before my kids did. My daughter has even taken to taunting me when she finds one, staying out of arm's length from me while she devours as many double chips as she can. On second thought, maybe we should try to get in the book for "Fastest

You Did What— with How Many People?

Here are some random examples of records from the *Guinness Book*. Share these with your children to get them excited about setting a record of their own.

Most hula hoops spun simultaneously	82
Youngest author	6 years old
Longest wheelchair journey	24,902.23 miles
Biggest "ring o' roses"	1,296 people
Lowest parachute escape (Don't try this one!)	39 feet
Most expensive bra	$10 million
Biggest chicken dance	72,000 people
Most body parts pierced	230 (175 on his face)
Biggest custard pie fight	3,312 pies in 3 minutes
Biggest Barbie (and Ken) doll collection	1,125

And don't forget my personal favorite: the record for the "Marshmallow Nose Blow." You'll have to look this one up yourself, but after you do, you might not want to see a marshmallow bobbing in your cup of hot cocoa ever again.

Scarfing Down of All Double-Folded Chips in a Super Size, 20-ounce Bag of Lay's Potato Chips." (I'm hoping that by listing Lay's in this story, the company will view it as a product placement, like in the movies, and they'll send me a check for a few million dollars . . . or at least a free bags of chips that I can sneak off with into the garage and consume all the doubles without fear of getting caught by my kids.)

Go ahead and try this on your own. Have fun with it.

By the way, did you know the answer to the question at the beginning of the chapter? The golden plover has been clocked at speeds of 40.4 MPH. But the grouse was the winner at 43.5 MPH.

36

All the Good Ideas Aren't Taken

Here's a way to have some one-on-one time with your kids—and maybe make a buck or two at the same time: Invent a product.

If you're like me, every time you hear about some new something coming out, you think, "Yeah! Why didn't I think of that?" The best way to come up with an invention is to look around the house or garage and consider what is it that you do on a regular basis that could use some new product or gadget to make your work easier. Believe me, it can be done. I wouldn't have believed it myself—except for the fact that I just did it.

My wife is a writer. In fact, one of her books was the inspiration for our invention. She has written a series of books titled *Secrets My Mom Never Taught Me*, one on cooking secrets, the second on housekeeping.

Before we go on, a quick aside on her cooking secrets book: My wife has won multiple cooking contests, and there are many incredible recipes and tips hidden within the pages of

Invent Away!

Do you have any ideas for a great, new product? Here are the steps you will need to take to make this idea a reality:

1. Brainstorm with your family and invent your product. (This is the fun part!)
2. If it's a physical item with moving parts, draw a diagram that shows how it works.
3. Build a prototype.
4. Test the prototype.
5. Come up with a name.
6. Look into a patent. (See the U.S. Patent Office Web site at www.uspt.gov.)
7. Call an advertising agency and see if you can pick someone's brain for marketing ideas.
8. Go for it!

her book. (I know what you're thinking, and this is absolutely *not* an attempt to get on my wife's good side!) Her book could be the catalyst for some cooking time together with you and your child. Even if you don't know the first thing about cooking, using this book you can become an expert on everything from pasta al dente to Yorkshire pudding, as well as what to prepare them in and how to clean up afterward. (For more on cooking with your kids, see chapter 8, "Over Easy or Sunny-Side Up?")

Actually, the cleanup is exactly where the housekeeping book comes in. I was reading a glowing review of the book in a New Orleans newspaper. The reviewer appreciated how my wife had not only identified each individual cleaning job, but also named the specific cleaner for it. I stopped counting product names at fourteen, turned to my wife, and said, "Why are we giving all of these mega-corporations free plugs for their products and making money for them? Why don't we invent our own cleaning product—one that does every job?" That's what got us started.

As we began to get serious about inventing an all-around cleaning product, our children started wondering what was going on at the Hilton house. When we told them what we were trying to do, it immediately became a family project.

First I found a chemical company that sells to individuals. Each step of the way, I let one of our children be a part of the creative and decision-making process. We'd have family discussions about what our product should and shouldn't do, what it should look like, how it should smell, and—the most fun part—what we should call it.

We spent weeks discussing names as we drove to school, to the market, to church, and to the chemical company. I won't repeat the plethora of names we considered, I'll just share the one we chose. I still believe my wife was joking when she first suggested this, but everyone cracked up when she said it, and I think it really works best. In the process of eliminating names, one of us would always pretend to clean, then turn to the other family members as though they were an audience and testify what a great job "product X" did. When I volunteered to demonstrate the name we ultimately chose, everyone laughed when I exclaimed the name of our product: "Holy Cow!" We laughed—but we loved the name.

It took a few days—and saying the new name a few thousand times—to really lock it in, but the real clincher for the name came when our daughter presented us with her drawing of a cow's face to use on the product label.

It was a great experience to watch my children when they visited the chemical company with me. They didn't just hang back intimidated; they asked questions and even made suggestions. The main point when doing any project with your kids is to treat them as equal partners. If you were operating with an adult partner, you'd listen to that person and discuss with him or her the best way to make your product work. If your children feel that you are taking their participation seriously, you'll see the light of pride in their eyes. And you'll feel it, too.

In the end it turned out that we couldn't use our daughter's drawing for the label. However, a commercial artist used her sketch for the prototype from which the final design was conceived.

When it came time to select the scent, all of our noses were involved, and after much sniffing and resniffing, we all agreed on the final bouquet.

The actual product testing, according to the children, wasn't very much fun. They saw through our "testing" ploy for what it really was: doing their regular household chores, but using only our new product for each job. Our oldest son really put the degreaser mix to the test when he used it to clean engine parts (and the street) while replacing the motor in his car.

Now we're working on an advertising campaign for our product. We've even made contact with QVC in the hopes of selling it through that channel.

Remember—this all started out as a wacky idea, and it may still end up that way, but playing mad scientist with each child has been fantastic. It would have been so easy to do this without their help, as adults do most of the time, but involving the kids has made our product stronger and forced us to think "outside the box." It was also great watching our children perform in an adult environment, watching them put into practice the life lessons we've taught.

Your idea for a new product may not take the same route as ours. You could suggest your kids "invent" a better way to feed their animals, clean their rooms, or just make time for all of you to sit around and talk about what they wish someone would invent. They won't even know that *this* is the best invention of all: a time machine.

37

Go Directly to Jail (Do Not Pass Go)

Not every adventure spent with your kids has to be fun or frivolous. Believe it or not, one of the standout times I had with my oldest son, who was thirteen at the time, was a trip to jail. I had been invited to spend the night in a newly completed city jail as part of a fund-raiser for the city. There were no real prisoners in the facility—just those like me who had paid to spend twenty-four hours there.

What began as a "cool" lark for my son slowly turned into a reality check—as in, "This isn't a place I *ever* want to be"— which is what I had hoped for. I watched my son's expression as he heard the cell doors lock each time we passed through and as we sat on the metal benches to eat bland meals served on metal trays, always at the mercy of the guards with regard to our requests for more food or even bathroom privacy. The night, spent trying to sleep on paper-thin mattresses laid out on knee-high concrete slabs, was tough enough without the added discomfort of lights left on for security's sake. By the time morning came we'd both had enough. Had it been possible, I would have gladly taken all four of my children with me on this adventure. Luckily the one who went painted a very vivid picture for the others of what "prison time" was all about. It was a great way to physically show my son—who in turn shared the experience with his siblings—the consequences for making certain wrong choices.

Although there may not be an opportunity for you to spend the night in jail (at least, I hope not), you can call your local police or sheriff's office to find out if it's possible to set up a jail tour for your kids. As part of the tour, they will "lock them up" for a moment to give them a brief glimpse of being behind bars.

Speaking of prison tours, another of my sons took a school field trip to one of the most infamous prisons, Alcatraz, nicknamed "The Rock." Today, the site is a national park, but the visit's impact on my son was tremendous nonetheless. When he came back he reported to us how the island had been taken over at one time by Native Americans, who were protesting violations of their civil rights by the U.S. government. He especially liked the audio tour, which walked them through the sights and history of The Rock. As my son said, "You feel as if the people, you know, the guards, the prisoners, you know, all of them, are talking to you, telling you about life there, the escapes, everything." The voices on the tape are the actual voices of some of the prisoners and guards who were there when it was a working prison.

If you're in the San Francisco area, load up on chocolates, stuff yourself with steamed crab and sourdough bread, watch the street performers, and check out the cable cars, the Golden Gate Bridge, and whatever else catches your eye, but make it a point to head out to Alcatraz. The boat departs from Pier 41; and reservations are required. For schedules, prices, and other information, go to www.blueandgoldfleet.com or call (415) 705-5555.

One last tip while we're on this "lock 'em up and throw away the key" theme: A friend of mine had a son who was arrested for speeding. When he asked me if I wanted to attend his son's hearing with him, I did. Wow! Was I shocked! If you want to give your kids a life lesson about how things they might consider to be "no big deal" really are, take them to court for a few hours and let them witness it firsthand.

While I was there I saw a pleasantly dressed, "girl next door" type called before the court. She explained to the judge that she was preparing to leave the state for college and asked for the court's forgiveness. She was in court for shoplifting a small, inconsequential item. Whether she could have afforded to buy the item she stole didn't matter. What did matter was that she was mortified, standing in front of a judge, bawling her eyes out, listening as the judge and the lawyer for the district attorney's office haggled over her fine and sentence. In the end, she got a fine—which far exceeded the price of the item she stole—and she was sentenced to do weekend litter pickup on the side of the road. On top of all that, she wasn't permitted to leave the state to attend the university she and her parents had more than likely worked so hard for so long to get her into.

It's the Law

For other ways to expose your children to the justice system, contact the public affairs division of your local police department, fire department, or SWAT team. Sometimes, these great folks will bring their vehicles to a neighborhood or school where kids can learn about safety, emergency procedures, and how much better the community is when everyone obeys the law. From bicycle safety and helmet use, to firework safety and the Fourth of July, to ways you can burglar-proof your home, to the services of the K-9 unit, they will present a fascinating program.

I watched others incur fines for "dumpster diving," and one man who was charged with assault for hitting another with a can of jalapeño peppers. Then there was the fisherman who was fined for having more fishing lines in the water than there were people in his boat, and another boater fined for letting two bikini-clad babes lounge on the front of his boat as he raced across the lake.

The judge charged one young driver with reckless driving, but added that she was willing to give him a suspended sentence, which meant he'd only have his license taken away for a short time. The kid, whose front porch light apparently wasn't burning very brightly that morning, replied (and I quote), "How can you take my license away when I don't have one?" If that wasn't stupid enough, he then turned around to look at his friends in the courtroom and chuckled. After a quick back pedal, the judge socked Einstein with a major fine and community service. And on and on and on it went.

Take your kids to court. It's cheaper than a movie and a better teacher than any book you'll ever read, even this one.

38

Alas, Poor Woody, We Knew Him Well

Not all activities you do with your children are fun. Take this story for instance, in which we learned about mourning. My daughter's guinea pig, Woody, died. This was all very sudden. We're still trying to figure out just what happened. One minute, he was fine, the next, he was lethargic, then he was gone. To a child, losing a pet can be as devastating as losing a human loved one. Teaching a child about death and dying is an important part of living. Times like this will help them cope in later life.

A short time before Woody died, I was working in the backyard when my wife came out to tell me our daughter wanted us to take Woody to the vet. We had already gotten him some antibiotics, but he still looked sluggish. Being the tender-hearted guy that I am, I reminded my wife that our daughter should pay for the vet visit out of her "income" (she walks the neighbors' dogs), because Woody was her own personal pet. (The rest of our menagerie belongs to the entire family.) When she originally asked if she could have the guinea pig, I told her yes, on the condition that she would earn the money for his food and any vet bills if she wanted to keep him. She agreed and did a fairly decent job of feeding, cleaning, and generally taking care of him.

When I came inside to remind her about our agreement, she stood before me, cheeks rosy red, eyes moist, chin trembling, and whispered something to me. I asked her what she had said and had to lean in close to hear her repeat her words.

"Daddy, I think Woody is dead."

My heart sank. My poor little girl was heartbroken. I felt terrible. How could I have been so mean as to delay even a moment getting her pet to the vet? (Of course, I didn't know it at the time, but my wife had already called around and found that there wasn't a vet who treated guinea pigs even available until the next day.)

I took my daughter back to her room to find, wrapped up in a little towel, the shiny, brown and white, chubby little guy that always let out little happy squeaks whenever anyone approached him. Only this time, he just lay there. I sat on the floor with my little girl, holding her, letting her cry against my shoulder, thinking about Toy.

Although it didn't seem that long ago, I was actually the same age my daughter is now. A car, speeding through our neighborhood, hit my dog Toy. He was the cutest, brightest, most energetic Boston terrier you'll ever meet. One of my neighbors came over to tell me he had witnessed the accident, but couldn't find Toy. I found him, whimpering underneath a bush on the side of our house. I grabbed some towels, wrapped them around Toy, and raced to the vet's office. I was a brand-new driver and I have absolutely no memory of how I got there. The vet examined my battered little friend and found that he had a punctured lung. Toy was shivering, barely able to stand on the shiny, cold operating table. He leaned against my chest as the doctor told me my pal would have to be put to sleep. I was already in such a state of shock that I didn't really comprehend what he meant. I was slowly rubbing Toy's back when I saw the vet give him a shot and watched as Toy crumpled lifeless to the table, right in front of my eyes. I screamed, "What have you done to my dog?" as my eyes seemed to explode with tears. He calmly told me that he had put him to sleep, just as he had told me he was going to do, and turned and walked out of the room. I felt dizzy, nauseated, and puzzled—but most of all angry. As I sit here writing this, I can still feel the emotions of that day. I also realized that I've never carried anger or disdain for anyone in my life—anyone except for that vet.

That night, as I watched my darling daughter's shoulders heave through her tears, I shared her pain. I made sure she knew how much I, too, liked her pal Woody. Her mom and I talked privately, making Woody's funeral arrangements. I asked my daughter if we could all go out together and find a place to bury him. She liked that idea. Time together, sharing pain. This time together comforting each other is as important, if not more so, than any other type of activity. This is a time she will never forget, and her memory will be one of having us there to comfort her for as long as she needs comforting, and also helping to bury her dear friend.

Saying Good-bye to a Family Pet

It's never fun to say good-bye to a family pet—especially when it dies, but even if it's been lost or has to be given or sent away. Participating in this process with your children helps them—and you—feel better about your loss and reinforces the love you feel as a family. Here are some ways to memorialize a beloved pet:

- Make a collage of pictures and words that describe how you felt about the pet. Hang it on the refrigerator or in the family room.

- If your pet's final resting place is your backyard, make a special headstone for the spot—paint on a rock, build a cross or other marker out of wood, or decorate it in a way that reminds you of that pet (using a dog's favorite toy or bone, for example).

- Talk about the pet with your kids. Tell them that you miss Sparky, or Princess, or Feathers, too. Let them know that you understand how hard it is to lose a furry—or feathered, or scaled—friend.

- Take time to make a toast to your departed pet at your next family dinner. Ask the pet's primary caretaker to say a few words, or have everyone around the table say what he or she will miss most about the pet.

By the time we had collected the flashlights, shovel, and found proper burial attire and an appropriate "casket" for Woody, it was late.

We drove down to the river and selected a quiet spot underneath a tree. I dug in silence as she held the light for me. I made sure the hole was deeper than necessary so that after the site was closed, other animals wouldn't seek out that spot. My daughter placed Woody in his little grave and we held a short prayer service. I asked her if she wanted to wait in the car as I replaced the sod on top of the small container, but she chose to stay there. As I finished, I made sure that I placed some of the vegetation over the top so that it could grow back to further disguise Woody's final resting place.

We were silent on the walk back to the car, her arm wrapped tightly around mine. The ride home was silent, too.

At bedtime, we recalled memories of Woody, about the fun and joy he brought into our lives.

You can never really plan for times like these. That's why all the time you spend together doing the other activities in this book are so important. They will help you build the foundation blocks that lead to a sweet, smiling face, staring up at you from her pillow, telling you, "Thanks for helping me tonight, Daddy. I love you."

A girl and her guinea pig. A boy and his dog. A daddy and his daughter. It's all about love.

39

Cannery
Chicanery!

I've always believed in involving children in service projects. If you've never done this with your children, you might begin by working through your church or civic organization, or just look through the paper and see who's doing what that might need you and your kids to help. We've done car washes and Christmas tree pickups as Scout projects, as well as taking food baskets to the needy and cleaning up a dilapidated cemetery with members of our church. In chapter 41, I write about taking my younger kids with me to serve food for the less fortunate at Thanksgiving. There are innumerable ways to offer service.

Don't assume that your kids will jump at the chance to volunteer for work projects when they could just as easily be doing something more "fun." The great thing about service, though, is that, for the most part, no matter how tough or how dirty the chore, a good feeling washes over everyone when all is said and done.

Take, for instance, the cemetery cleanup. It was held on a hot, muggy August afternoon. As one of my church's youth leaders, I had nearly called off the event because we had hit record highs of around 110 degrees the previous day. We stuck with our plan, though, and as it turned out, the temperature stayed in the nineties on cleanup day (hot enough, I'd say), thanks in no small part to a little bit of "Delta breeze." The sound of weed whackers, lawn mowers, shovels hitting hard soil, and young people yelling and singing began to fill the air. Chatter floated across the hill as the kids cleaned tombstones, revealing names and dates. You could hear the respectful tones as the boys and girls began to feel the spirits of those long ago buried at this spot. They realized the historic dates they studied in school actually applied to the lives of those buried there.

After helping with the cleanup work, my son soon joined me at the bottom of the hill, where I had set up the barbecue for the burgers and dogs we were going to serve the workers at the end of the day. My son told me about the tombstones he'd cleaned, and I could tell he was particularly affected by those of children who had died before reaching the age he was at the time. The day turned out to be one of the best youth events I'd ever participated in, and I was so thankful I hadn't canceled it.

Another time I took one of my sons to a church-owned cannery, where all the processing and canning is done on a strictly volunteer basis. What a once-in-a-lifetime experience that was! As you might expect, the cannery was located in an industrial area and looked pretty much like any other building, at least from the outside. Once inside, we were given safety instructions, lab coats, gloves, boots, hairnets, and goggles. We all looked as if we were contestants on a really bad game show.

The night's assignment was canning chicken pieces. Some teams hosed the cement floor down to keep it free of bits of chicken other debris, others sent empty cans down the conveyor line, and others hovered over huge round vats of chicken meat (we were in this group). We had to put a specified amount of chicken meat and a little water in each can as it came around the perimeter of the vat on the conveyor, held in place by a metal railing. The process was nonstop—unless the cans jammed, which happened from time to time. It was monotonous work, so we did what we could to amuse ourselves. I stood nearest the "topping" area, the place where, after you used your gloved hand to compress the chicken, the machinery grabbed the can for the lids to be placed on top and sealed. The steam from the hot water hose gave the room an eerie look, especially with all of the overhead pipes running across the low ceiling. It started to feel as though we were on some old, rickety Russian trawler—or at least how I imagined an old Russian trawler might look. For some reason, I began to act out the part of a Russian prisoner being forced to do this work; my son played along, pretending to be my Russian guard. Pretty soon, we had the whole crew laughing and forgetting how mindless the work was. It turned out to be a rather fun evening after all.

The best part of that work project occurred several months later, when I discovered that the food we canned that night had been sent to recent earthquake victims in Nicaragua, people who had no idea that a son and father another world away had spent the night laughing together so that they wouldn't go hungry after enduring a cataclysmic event.

Manners, Please

Here are some quick ways to give your kids a leg up in social situations, and even a jump start for future job interviews:

- Have a firm (but not too firm) handshake.
- Make, and maintain, eye contact.
- Speak up; don't mumble.
- Don't slouch; maintain good posture.
- Even work clothes should be as neat and clean as possible.
- Respond to all adults with "yes sir/ma'am" and "no sir/ma'am."
- Have energy.
- Smile.

Teach your children the importance of service by participating in service projects together. Show them that giving back is what lives, hopes, and dreams are built on. When the people we help are later on given the chance to help others, don't you think they'll grab their kids and take it? That, my friend, is what is known as the circle of life.

40

Triskaidekaphobia!

In this chapter, you'll learn some history, so you can share it with each of your children (especially the younger ones) in a one-on-one session. Fear not, I explain the meaning of the chapter title in the box "Lucky Thirteen" on page 202. I'm going to give you some information about the beginnings and design of that little piece of green paper that runs through our hands entirely too fast: the one dollar bill. I found many of these facts on the Internet and did my best to verify, or at least clear up, some of the hazier points of the most widely believed version of the dollar's history.

First, grab a kid (one of your own) and go buy something: a burger, some ice cream, a movie ticket, whatever. Make sure to give the cashier enough money so that you get back at least one dollar bill in change. Look longingly at the currency, sigh, and then (presuming that you have memorized the following), sit down with your child and tell him the story of the dollar bill.

Hold on to your wallet, and away we go. The dollar bill first came off the presses in its current design in 1957. It's printed on high-quality paper that's a blend of cotton and linen, with red and blue silk fibers running through it. That's why you can run it through a load of laundry and it doesn't fall apart (unlike your kids' report cards). The ink used to print money is a special, secret blend. The bill is also overprinted with symbols, starched to make it water resistant, and then pressed to make it crisp. On the front of the bill, as most kids will already know, is the picture of our first president, George Washington. If you look to ol' George's left, you'll see the seal of the U.S. Treasury. The scales on top of the seal represent the solemn task given Congress—that of balancing the budget. In the center of the seal is a chevron with thirteen stars representing the original colonies. Near the bottom of the seal is a key, which represents the treasury's authority to issue bills.

The rest of the dollar bill's front side is pretty self-explanatory, so flip it over in a dramatic gesture and say something like, "If you think that's something, wait'll I tell you what's on *this* side!"

First, point out the two circles. These depict the front and back of the great seal of the United States of America. The first Congress asked Ben Franklin, John Adams, Thomas Jefferson, and two others to design the great seal, but it actually took six years—and the efforts of a total of fourteen men—before the final design was accepted.

In the left-hand circle is a pyramid. The face of the pyramid is lighted, but its western side is dark. This is the only unsubstan-

Lucky Thirteen

So what does the number thirteen have to do with the dollar bill—or, for that matter, U.S. history? As you've already read, there are several symbols on the dollar bill that represent our nation's original thirteen colonies. But that's not all. Many people say the number thirteen is unlucky and fear it. In fact, that's what the name of this chapter—triskaidekaphobia—means: a fear of the number thirteen. (It's pronounced tris-kai-dek-uh-FO-bee-uh.) That's why you rarely, if ever, see a room 13 or a thirteenth floor in a hotel. But take a look at the other side of thirteen:

- Thirteen original colonies
- Thirteen signers of the Declaration of Independence
- Thirteen stripes on our flag
- Thirteen steps on the pyramid in our nation's great seal
- Thirteen letters in the Latin above the pyramid (on the dollar)
- Thirteen letters in "E Pluribus Unum"
- Thirteen stars above the eagle
- Thirteen bars on the shield
- Thirteen leaves on the olive branch
- Thirteen fruits on the olive branch (break out the magnifying glass for this one)
- Thirteen arrows

Oh, and let's not forget the 13th Amendment to the U.S. Constitution, which abolished slavery.

tiated part of this lesson, but it is thought that the designers meant this as symbolism to show that our country was just beginning and Western expansion hadn't really started. Point out to your children that the pyramid is uncapped, signifying that we were just getting started as a nation. The pyramid signifies strength and duration. The eye inside the pyramid's capstone is known as the Eye of Providence, an ancient symbol for divinity. In keeping with this theme, the seal committees voted to include the phrase "In God We Trust." Above the pyramid is the Latin phrase "Annuit Coeptis," which means "God has favored our undertaking." The Latin below the pyramid, "Novus Ordo Seclorum," means "A new order for the ages." And at the bottom of the pyramid are the Roman numerals MDCCLXXVI, which stand for 1776.

On the right-hand circle is the symbol that's depicted on every national cemetery in the United States. It is also on the Parade of Flags walkway at the National Cemetery in Bushnell, Florida. With slight modifications, this is also the same seal the president uses to decorate the podium whenever and wherever he speaks. The major difference between the seal on the dollar and the seal the president uses is the way the eagle's head turns. In 1945, President Harry Truman ordered that the eagle's head be turned away from the arrows and toward the olive branch, indicating that we are a nation of peace first and foremost.

The designers of the seal chose the bald eagle because of its association with victory, strength, and wisdom, and its ability to soar above any storms. The eagle wears no material crown. This was important because we had just broken away from the king of England.

The shield in front of the eagle stands unsupported as a testament that our country can stand on its own. The shield—originally drawn in red, white, and blue—symbolizes the unity of a new nation.

In the eagle's beak is a banner that reads "E Pluribus Unum," which means "One from many." Above the eagle are thirteen stars representing the thirteen colonies. In its talons the eagle holds an olive branch on one side and arrows on the other, signifying that as a nation we prefer peace but are unafraid to fight should it become necessary.

What do you think? I think this information will knock your kids' socks off, and you'll come off looking like quite the scholar. This might also get your kids excited about American history and about being an American citizen.

Who says you can't get anything for a buck these days?

41

If Ye Have Faith As a Grain of Mustard Seed

The holidays present a great way to spend time with your kids and do some needed community service at the same time. Check your local newspaper, church bulletins, and even the bulletin boards at your local markets for opportunities to volunteer at soup kitchens, homeless shelters, and other places where they feed the needy. These agencies are always looking for extra hands during the busy holiday mealtimes.

I found our service opportunity in the city section of our local newspaper, which listed several Thanksgiving holiday festivals. A community center in a less-affluent neighborhood needed volunteers for one of its meal services. After calling the number to check it out and hearing back the next day that they still needed volunteers, I decided to take my two younger children with me. I had hoped that the kids could help dish out the food as the folks progressed through the buffet line, but when we arrived at the appointed day and time, they asked us instead to help out in the clothing room. Several banquet tables had been set up to hold the piles of donated clothing that would be passed out, free, to those in need after the meal.

My son took direction and quickly began unloading boxes and bags of shoes, ties, pants, dresses, suits, shirts, and other items. My daughter wasn't so quick to get to work and surveyed the unfamiliar scene a bit timidly. She sidled over to me at one point and whispered, "When can we leave?" I whispered back to her, "As soon as you've completed your assignment." And then a thought hit me, so I shared it with her: "There is probably someone here right now, or someone who is coming here later, who is in need of help that only you can give. It would be a shame if we left without finishing what we came here to do."

That seemed to appease her. Soon enough, we finished our work in the clothing area, so I asked if we could head over to the gymnasium where they were going to feed everyone. When we got there, all the assignments had been given out except for serving coffee and juice. We grabbed some empty cake boxes to use as serving trays.

Before they let the hungry folks in, the group running the event started things off with a prayer to dedicate this service project. The church we regularly attend is a joyful and happy place and we, too, pray to give thanks or dedicate our services—but this group was a bit more boisterous than what we were accustomed to. Growing up in the deep South, I was reared on gospel music and fervent church meetings, but my children had never been exposed to that kind of thing. As the speaker delivered the opening prayer, he became more and more excited (and his voice grew louder and louder), so did

How to Help

When looking for ways to volunteer, an easy place to begin is with your city's yellow pages. Look under Health Service, Charities, Human Services, Social Services, and government listings for places where you can help out. Common volunteer activities include:

- Serving meals
- Painting and repairing
- Sorting clothing
- Stuffing envelopes
- Manning the phones
- Preparing emergency kits
- Collecting canned goods
- Distributing toys
- Landscaping and building
- Distributing fliers
- Giving comfort

This is just the tip of the iceberg. There are many other ways you can volunteer your time and effort.

many of the others in the gym. With eyes shut, I smiled as I remembered listening to such reveling as a boy. I was startled to feel two anxious little hands squeeze mine. The panicked looked in my daughter's eyes jolted me back to reality. I realized that she had never been to any worship services or church events other than her own, and this was quickly becoming a service unlike any she had ever seen. She mouthed, "I'm scared; let's go." I just patted her hand and put my arm around her to let her know that everything was fine.

As the doors opened and hungry people began to file in, I made sure my daughter kept busy, helping to fill the cups with punch while I poured the coffee, and then walking with me and offering drinks to the people as they sat down with their food. I made sure both children showed complete respect to those they served, calling them "Sir" or "Ma'am" and thanking *them* for being there. Soon I saw a change take place in my daughter as she stopped worrying about herself and concentrated on helping others. It wasn't long before she quit waiting for me to help her serve, and went off on her own, filling and distributing cups herself.

As my children worked independently of me, I watched in awe as they soothed and comforted rough-looking men, sadlooking women, and desperate-looking children. At one point, the gospel music stopped and a singer from the gospel group stepped forward. She announced that she was going to sing the national anthem. I thought it strange, both in song choice and in timing, but I was wrong on both counts. As she sang, I felt chills come over me, her voice penetrating right to my core. I looked around and watched rugged men, tired men, fearsomelooking men—the kind of men you might choose to walk the other way from if you saw them on a dark street—now unabashedly wiping tears away as this angel's voice lilted through the hall. At the conclusion of her song, the room was perfectly quiet. Then another singer stepped forward as music filled the room again. Accompanied by soft, prerecorded background music, the woman walked through the crowd carrying a wireless microphone, singing a hymn about hope—and how fortunes can change if they only had faith as a grain of mustard seed. As she sang, she reached out to each person with her right hand, handing him or her a tiny seed, a mustard seed that she plucked from her other hand. I saw smiles return as each person received this marvelous gift, a gift so small you could hardly see it, but so big that it filled their hearts with hope. I watched as one man clenched his calloused, bruised hand around his little mustard seed, his eyes rimmed with tears. I felt tears moving down my own face and I turned so that no one would see me. But someone did. My daughter. Turns out, I was the person who needed her help that day. She put her little arms around my waist to comfort me, patting me. As the afternoon deepened and the crowds began to thin out, we were invited to join in the feast of leftover food. My daughter smiled her "missing most of her teeth" smile and asked if we could "pleeeeezzzzzze stay, Daddy?"

What a day that was. Earlier, when she was whining and asking to leave, I wondered if I had made a mistake bringing her. I felt I had not, but I wasn't sure. I guess all I needed was a little faith . . . as a grain of mustard seed. Oh, by the way, I approached the singer and held out my hand, and now I have my own mustard seed to carry with me always.

42

The Confusing Case of the Corncob Pipe

Genealogy. Family history. Skeletons in the closet. However you might want to define it, searching for one's roots is a wonderful way to spend time with your children and a fabulous chance to teach them about their ancestors. Not everyone has a famous (or, as the case may be, infamous) person in his or her lineage, but the search itself can be fun for everyone—and a great way to get to know each other. (For some ways to get started, see "Uncover the Skeletons in Your Closet," page 214.) The discoveries you and your children make about history and family ties, ancient and more recent, will be invaluable.

Once you've done some research, you may even want to take a trip to the land, state, county, or city where your ancestors lived. My cousin Sharon began her search as a lark to identify some of the people in photographs hanging on the wall of our grandmother's home when we were kids. This has sparked a family hobby that continues even now that she and her husband are retired empty nesters. They sold their home, bought a motor home, and now travel the country to wherever the genealogy trail takes them.

My family is also caught up in a similar search, but on a smaller scale. It began with a curious boy, me, trying to find out about a corncob pipe that has been in our family. My grandfather told me the pipe belonged to one of our relatives, a Thomas Sumter. General Thomas Sumter. Yes, *that* Sumter, for whom Fort Sumter, where the first shot of the Civil War was fired, was named. (To clear up one point, Sumter is the spelling used by the general and the fort, but *our* part of the family added a "p" to the name: Sumpter. No one knows when or why the change was made.)

As they got old enough to care, I have told each child about the story of the corncob pipe and their famous relative, General Thomas Sumter.

For Christmas several years ago my wife surprised me with an incredible gift. The first part of the gift was an out-of-print book, *Gamecock*, about the life and times of General Thomas Sumter. (I'll get to the second part of the gift in a minute.) I was absolutely stunned, holding in my hands actual proof of this ancestor whose life I had only imagined until now. I gathered my children around me and read to them about this famous man. My children's eyes sparkled as they learned how he garnered a reputation for being a "wild man" early on, how he loved gambling, cock fighting, and horse racing. (A lecture on the wrongs of each activity was also included.) When I got to parts about his natural ability as a fighter and a warrior, the kids sat riveted as I turned each page. The men Sumter fought with and against were impressive: Light Horse Harry Lee, Lord Cornwallis, King Charles X, Indian Chief Ostenaco, Governor Dinwiddie, "Swamp Fox" Francis Marion, George Washington, and other presidents, kings, and figures of the Revolution.

Sumter was nicknamed the Gamecock for the way he fought, apparently enjoying the blood of the fight as much as he savored the victory. I led the children through his war campaigns, fighting with the Continental Army, leading guerrilla fighters, running the state of South Carolina while it was without a governor, being promoted to general, and eventually being elected to the U.S. Senate.

General Sumter, the last surviving general of the American Revolution, lived to the ripe old age of ninety-eight, riding horseback daily until his dying day, on which he sat down in his favorite chair, his head slumped forward, and died.

The second part of the gift, which had been hidden in the garage and was now leaning against the fireplace, came in a huge package, 5 feet by 3 feet, wrapped in brown paper with a giant red bow. When I carefully unwrapped the gift, I could hardly believe it. In the midst of seemingly tons of discarded paper I discovered an enormous oil painting of a man dressed in revolutionary military clothing. He stood on a precipice, his right arm cocked, his right hand resting on hip, his left arm proudly jutting straight out, his left hand grasping the handle of his sword, forcing the point of the weapon down into the earth. His bright blue jacket, trimmed in gold, matched his gold trousers, which were tucked into his knee-high black riding boots. Most first-time observers of the painting guess the figure in the frame to be that of George Washington. At first glance, however, I immediately recognized my grandfather's cheekbones, nose, and eyes.

My wife had discovered the existence of the original painting of General Sumter through several phone conversations with curators at the Sumter Court House. She hired someone to take a color slide of the painting and then had an artist friend reproduce the magnificent gift for me.

The stories passed down through time about General Sumter, real or imagined, have been the source of some wonderful moments for my children and me. Nowhere in any of the research have I found any factual evidence that the aforementioned corncob pipe, now in a Sumpter cousin's possession, ever belonged to the general. But the time we've spent together researching our family history is as important, if not more so, than the truth, whatever it might be.

To this day, the huge portrait of General Thomas Sumter (no "p") hangs over our fireplace mantel, even though research by my mean cousin Sharon basically shows that our line and the general's aren't as direct as we first thought. It looks as if we might be related through the general's brother William, though we still have no clue as to the owner of the pipe. However, that hasn't stopped the kids from talking about our "famous" ancestor, even telling first-time visitors to our home that the guy in the tight gold pants in the painting over the mantel is some guy from Dad's past. I guess this means I'll need to work twice as hard now to make a connection between me and the Hilton Hotel part of the family! It's worth a try.

Uncover the Skeletons in Your Closet

So how do you go about uncovering your own history? There are books galore, other library resources, family bibles with marriage and death records, even some churches with genealogical libraries. The Church of Jesus Christ of Latter-day Saints (the Mormon church) has the most extensive resources, it's free, and you don't have to be a member to research it. Best of all, it's all on the Internet at www.familysearch.org.

In fact, if you hit your favorite Web search engine and type in the word "genealogy," you'll uncover more resources than you'll know what to do with. You can also go through the Daughters or Sons of the Revolution (DAR and SAR). There is a patriot lookup service on the DAR Web site (www.dar.org) that allows you to do a free search for relatives who may have participated in the American Revolution. If you use this search service, you will need the birth and death dates and locations for the relative you want to check out, his or her wartime residence, and his or her spouse's name.

One way to make this more interesting for young children, since they like to actually see and touch things, is to draw your family tree. You can buy a blank diagram at a craft or stationery store, or have the children create their own (you'll find tips on how to do this online, too). As they discover relatives—or reprobates—they can fill in the blanks by writing in names or by drawing characters for the newfound family members.

43

Signs of the Time

In an earlier chapter, I suggested taking a class with your child. One suggestion was to study another language. Although some school districts across the country offer languages as a part of the curriculum, it's usually in the later grades rather than the elementary grades when children tend to pick up languages more easily and permanently. For this reason, you do your children and yourself a favor by taking language classes with them at the earliest age possible—even as early as they can understand words. In this chapter, however, the language I want to focus on is not spoken at all. It's sign language. More specifically, American Sign Language, or ASL.

No one is sure exactly when or where formal sign language came in to being. In 1620, Juan Pablo de Bonet published the first book on teaching sign language to the deaf that included a manual (sign) alphabet. A little over a hundred years later, in 1755, a French abbot named Charles Michel de L'Epée founded the first free school for the deaf in Paris. He also created a language of signs in which each gesture stood for a word or concept. To do this, he studied the signs that a group of Parisian deaf people used and added his own signs to this new language. American Sign Language is based on de L'Epee's system—today known as French Sign Language—which Thomas Gallaudet brought to America in 1816. He also brought a French teacher named Laurent Clerc with him. Together, they opened the first American school for the deaf in Hartford, Connecticut, the following year.

There are now hundreds of schools for the deaf and thousands of books that teach people how to sign. And yet few hearing people have any idea what this language is all about, or how to sign even the most basic letters or words. Have you seen that commercial on TV—the actual product escapes me now—that depicts a neighbor bringing a pie to welcome a new family to the neighborhood? On discovering that the child of the couple is deaf, the well-meaning neighbor tries to learn a few words in sign language. But as she attempts to sign, "Welcome to the neighborhood" and hand the boy the pie, his eyes widen in fear and he takes off, running away from her. Meanwhile, the closed caption shows that the words she signed indicated that she wanted to hurt his dog.

The commercial is meant to be cute, of course, but wouldn't it be neat to learn a little of this visual language and spend some one-on-one time with your child at the same time?

One of the sweetest moments for me this past holiday season took place at the Christmas program at my daughter's school. After the fourth- and fifth-grade band struggled through some simple holiday songs, my daughter's fourth-grade

A Good Sign

How do you learn sign language? You can pick up a book, go to a school, or find lots of resources on the Internet (a good place to start is the American Sign Language Teachers Association Web site: www.aslta.org). You could also try asking your children. They often know more than we do about the things that are really important. Here's a quick sign language phrase to use when your child comes home from school today: Bend your right arm toward your chest, your hand in the shape of a fist, the thumb touching your chest, with your little finger raised skyward. That's the first word. Make the next word by crossing both arms over your chest with your hands open, palms flat over your heart. Last, point your right index finger directly at your child. They will understand what you're saying.

I developed a similar gesture when all of my children were little. If they were leaving with my wife or I was heading off to work, I'd point at my left eye with my right index finger, then I'd tap my chest over my heart, and then I'd point at them. To this day, the minute I begin this motion, it's returned, not just in kind, but in kind . . . with a smile.

Learn sign language with your children. I'm working on it, too.

chorus—angels' voices all—happily chirped through their medley. Next, the lights dimmed and the familiar strains of "Silent Night" started to play over the school's sound system. Suddenly, out of the darkness, there appeared onstage forty pairs of small hands wrapped in fluorescent gloves, shaping the words of this beloved song in sign language. The audience full of parents immediately applauded the clever staging of the song. But after a moment, the sound of applause dissolved into quiet as the song continued and the magnitude of what these tiny children were doing—and the spirit in which it was being done—hit each and every one of us. Those fourth-graders' relatively small gesture made such an incredible difference that evening. That night, instead of the usual facetious congratulations for "such a remarkable performance," parents beamed with genuinely proud faces and moist eyes. And the children knew they had indeed given a truly remarkable performance.

44

Gone Fishin'

I'm surprised at how many adults have memories of going
fishing with their fathers. And these folks aren't even fishing
experts. In fact, they hardly know the difference between bob-
bers and sinkers, hooks and lines. If you're in this category, and
you'd like to try a weekend of fishing with your child . . . piece
of cork. There is not a city, town, or village that doesn't have a
fishing store, or at least a sporting goods store with a fishing
equipment department—and salespersons who consider themselves experts on the sport. They will tell you the best lines,
poles, bait, and a million other things they claim you need for
your outing. They will also tell you *how* to be a champion fisherman. But, really, all you need is your kid, a pole, the ol' hook,
line, and sinker—and a good attitude.

Out of all her memories of adventures with her father, my
mother named fishing as her favorite. My grandfather was a
man who, among other things, ran a sawmill in Louisiana in
the early 1900s and used the cooling pond as a swimming pool

for local kids. Not known for his charity among the neighbors, my granddad charged the kids to swim. The only reason they put up with it was because, back in that day, his was one of the very few places boys and girls were allowed to swim together—which made some less-than-pleased parents want to put a few buckshot in the backside of my granddad's lap. If you look up the word "irascible" in the dictionary . . . you'll probably find my grandfather's picture. But he took my mother fishing.

I recently flew to Louisiana to meet my brother to investigate the theft of some timber on a backwoods parcel of property that had been in our family for years. It turned out that one of our infamous cousins had strip-cut not just our lots, but also the adjoining lots of several other relatives years before—but then, that's another story. When my brother and I discovered that there was nothing we could do (the statute of limitations ran from commission of the crime and not from the date of discovery), we decided to take a trip down memory lane. We visited many of places we remembered from childhood (Louisiana's not that big). One of these spots was Toro Creek, where Mom and my grandfather had fished. In Mom's memory, it had been a huge, raging creek with dirt banks ten feet high. In reality, it was no bigger than the manmade stream that flows through the lobby of the Hyatt Regency near Fisherman's Wharf in San Francisco. My grandfather was a crab most of the time, but to hear my mother talk about him taking her fishing, you'da thunk he had walked on the water they cast their lines into.

My wife has great memories of fishing with her father. She remembers the whisper of the wind as it rippled through the canyons, making the leaves of the quaking aspen trees shiver.

She smiles as she recalls a vision of a fish, dripping with water, dancing in its last throes of bravado as she and her father pulled it out of the stream, then the smell of butter crackling in the frying pan, followed by the taste of fresh rainbow trout. Even the fright of a bear that chased them back to their car and proceeded to severely damage the vehicle in an attempt to steal their fish didn't dampen her sweet memories. Of course, she also remembers her dad constantly shushing her (apparently, my wife was a *very* talkative child) in an attempt to teach her to be quiet, to enjoy nature, and most of all, *not* to frighten the fish away.

People have told me stories of deep-sea fishing trips, lake trips, lost rods and reels, no catches—not all fishing memories are people's favorites. One friend told me that her memory of fishing with her father wasn't fun at all. He made her and her sister hold lighted cigarettes on each side of him to help keep the bugs away, occasionally requiring them to puff on the cigarettes to create more smoke. She says she laughs about it now—and that the experience is probably the reason she never took up smoking when all of her peers did. (See? From the bad comes some good.)

When we lived in Southern California, I decided to be a pioneer pop and take one of my sons fishing. There are beaucoup places to fish in the State of California, but I didn't know where any good spots were locally, so I looked in the yellow pages under *Fishing*. I found a place close by that touted its fresh flowing mountain water and guaranteed you'd catch your limit of beautiful rainbow trout. I called for more information and the trip was on. We left the next day at the crack of noon, drove twelve-and-a-half miles, and there it was. Sort of. Next to me sat my very excited son ready to catch "the big one," and laid out in front of me, crammed between two huge new housing developments, was a poorly fenced, run-down, park-like area guarded by a bored, bearded, derelict-looking guy in a shabby kiosk. Of course he was charging for parking, poles . . . and anything else he could get away with. After deciding there was no easy way to explain to a four-year-old why we weren't going fishing today after all, I paid the parking fee and our adventure began. At the back of the property, I discovered two ancient, crumbling cement "ponds" being aerated by large black hoses connected to an irritatingly loud pump. Beside each gurgling, polluted-looking tank, signs told you there were small fish (cheaper) in the tank on the right and larger fish (more expensive) in the one on the left. The place charged by the inch for the fish you caught—whether you kept them or not. The bait was cheese. That's right, slices of regular old American cheese. The rapscallion at the kiosk told me to break off a piece of cheese, then roll it between my thumb and fingers, squeezing it into a ball that I could then put the hook through. The first piece of cheese was free, but I had to buy another piece after my son ate the first slice. (We had not yet gone over the difference between fish bait and snack food.)

Finally, time to fish. Once we "baited" our hook, we plopped the line into the "fishin' hole," hoping to catch—rather than knock out—a fish. I looked around and saw the embarrassed looks on the faces of other dads, caught just like me at the 7-Eleven of fishing spots. I decided to go back to the ticket seller and asked if he might have some *real* bait, and for another

Fishing Tips for Beginners

If you're hoping to get expert fishing tips from me, you're casting into the wrong pond. Check your yellow pages under "Fishing Guides." They can teach you all you want to know. However, if you are in the same angler category as I am, here are some tips you can use:

1. Make sure you put the tip of the hook through the middle of the corn kernel, not your finger. Trout don't like blood on their food.

2. Bring a pair of needle-nose pliers to extract the hook from the fish's mouth—or your pants, whichever comes first.

3. To cast, lift the pole with the tip skyward, swing the corn-impaled hook toward the water and do your best to drop it into the pond rather than on the ground.

4. Most important, bring a camera. A picture of a child and his or her first catch is forever—even if it is not at a real fishing hole.

dollar, he handed me a small ketchup cup with about eighteen soggy corn kernels in it. If it had been possible to feel more foolish than I already did, that would have been the time.

Without a doubt, this seemed like the stupidest idea that I had ever invested my time and money in—and if you've read the other chapters in this book, you know there are some whoppers in my past. I dreaded going home and telling my wife about this faux fishing hole. (Plus, I didn't know if the local market even carried fresh rainbow trout.)

But guess what? The moment my son hooked a fish and started whooping and hollering, I could feel the surging power of the great Colorado River raging at our feet. We fought this monster of the deep, our rod and reel bending like a great willow against the orca on the other end, our waders filling with the freezing waters of the runoff from the snow-capped mountains above. In reality, the fish was too small to take home, and it cost more to toss it back into the murky kiddie pool than it did to keep it, but my son was ecstatic. It was the biggest fish he'd ever caught. (I know, I know, it was the *only* fish he'd ever caught, but that didn't matter at the moment.) And then it was as if nothing else mattered. He had caught the fish that he came to catch, and now all he wanted to do was watch the turtles on the side of the pond, leaving me with two cane poles, seventeen pieces of corn, and a half-slice of bad cheese. (Fishing tip: We caught our guppy using corn. No bites on the cheese.)

At least he didn't hate the trip. The market did have fresh rainbow trout (boned and gutted!). And I've saved the phone number and address of that wilderness wonderland in the event he turns out to be a great outdoorsman like his father.

Take your kids fishing. How much worse could it be?

45

Congratulations! You May Be a Winner!

Here's a fun, potentially profitable—but possibly fattening— way to spend time with your children. Enter contests! The fattening part comes in because I'm talking primarily about cooking contests. Don't run and hide just because you don't cook. It isn't as tough an assignment as it might sound, and the prizes are often surprisingly generous. Many contests pay thousands and thousands of dollars in addition to giving away things like computer systems, stoves, refrigerators, and more. The mother of all prizes, of course, is $1 million from Pillsbury. Hey, somebody has to win this stuff—why not you and your child?

First things first. You need to find out what your children like to eat. I know mine—and perhaps yours—often seem like bottomless food-processing machines, but if you sit them down and get past the Krispy Kremes and Burger Kings, you might be surprised to find an actual palate under their M&M-laced breath.

Once you've decided to try this with your little rascals, make sure you have a pad of paper and something to write with, and then start making notes—muffins, pies, cakes, main courses, and so on. As an example, in our family one child loves cherry pies while another hates any type of fruit pies but adores chocolate. Another likes only key lime pie, and the fourth— bring it on, anything is "fare game" to him.

After you have your list of desirable foods, hit the Net. You want to find out what companies make the products that they like, then hone in on those companies' Web sites, which will almost always include—somewhere in the midst of the product propaganda—contest information that explains how to enter, the rules of that particular contest, and any purchase requirements.

We've done this many times and have had a bit of luck (though, of course, the real prize is time with your child). We entered a contest sponsored by Dreyer's/Edy's Grand brand of ice cream. The contest called for creating an ice cream flavor using a racing theme. The contest judge was to be the man himself, NASCAR grand champion Jeff Gordon. Wow! The idea was to create a new flavor, using Dreyer's/Edy's Grand ice cream of course, that would, somehow, have a NASCAR feel. They were looking for "Jeff's next flavor."

Our family loves ice cream—absolutely adores it. My wife and I even briefly considered opening our own frozen custard stand (that's ice cream that's creamier, richer, better-tasting, less fattening, and made with eggs in the batter) but decided the timing wasn't right. Maybe later, maybe never. I really think the idea of operating our own place appealed to us because we knew we could eat as much as we wanted, anytime we wanted, without the worry of some kid at a cash register saying, "You're back—again?"

Anyway . . . our son entered this contest and was selected as one of five finalists out of more than 8,000 entries. He won a trip to the company's ice cream factory in Texas, where he would assemble his concoction so Jeff Gordon could judge the five finalists' entries. The grand prize was the chance to attend the Texas 300 NASCAR race in Dallas as Jeff's guest.

My son's entry was called "Cool Fuel," a mixture of "cool, minty ice cream with streaks of fudge injected (racing term to sway the judge) with almonds." Before the final judging, there were many (free) ice cream samplings and tours of the factory. We didn't win, but we did get pit passes for the race and a chance to visit Jeff's racing trailer and meet his crew. Wait a minute! Did I say we didn't win? Listen to the prize for the runner-up. All kinds of cool Jeff Gordon stuff, including two autographed hats, a plaque, and, best of all, a two-year supply of ice cream (which we ate in six months' time). I'd say we won, wouldn't you?

The idea with this activity is to try. Add an ingredient here, another there, make changes in family recipes to see what works. But you can't win if you don't at least try. My daughter and I just got a letter informing us that we are finalists in an oat contest. I don't know if we will win or not, but the fun we had making our oat muffins (she handled the recipe, I took care of cleanup) was a prize in and of itself.

In a month or so, the winner will be announced, but by that time, we'll have started on bananas, caramel corn, or maybe even cookies to try to best those little elves. Are we nerv-

Contest Search

To find out which companies sponsor contests for kids, hit the Web and simply go to each company's Web site. Some companies that make products kids love are:

Nabisco

Keebler

Oscar Mayer

Dreyer's/Edy's Ice Cream

Eggo

Nestle

Kraft

Green Giant

General Mills

Skippy Peanut Butter

Jell-O

Quaker

Pillsbury

Kellog's

Hershey's

Don't forget to check Internet links with the words "recipe" and "cooking contest." And remember organizations that represent whole industries, such as dairy products, pork, and so on.

ous about this oat contest? Do we really care which prize we win? Let me see . . . several thousand dollars and a new video room—or $25 and a box of oats. Hmmmm! You decide.

Excuse my greed. That's not the point. And, in fact, it wasn't. We had a ball, gained three pounds, and are already laughing at the prospect of what we're going to make out of the box of oats we used to cook with.

Want to have some tasteful fun? Enter a contest with your child.

46

It's All Ben Franklin's Fault

Ifigured this chapter would be a slam dunk. Here's the activity: Grab your kid and go fly a kite. The end, right? Well, it turns out there's a whole lot more to it than that. (As I'm sure Ben Franklin can attest.)

I've never been much of a kite flier. Before I started researching this chapter, my thought was: Take four pieces of inch-wide baseboard and nail them together in a diamond pattern. Then, attach two smaller sticks in a cross pattern to the splintery wooden diamond. Cover that with a sheet of newspaper (any section but the comics—otherwise your kids will spend all of their time trying to read the kite), attach a roll of twine, and, for the tail, add the tie your kid made for you at his last Cub Scout pack meeting. Voila! You've got a kite. This is not to say that I've ever made one, or even successfully gotten a real one to fly. I'm what you might call the Charlie Brown of kite flying.

If kite flying interests you as an activity, check out the Web site for the American Kitefliers Association at www.aka

.kite.org. This 4,000-member nonprofit organization's purpose is to educate interested persons "in the art, history, technology, and practice of building and flying kites." The organization purports to have men, women, and children in more than thirty-five countries who are interested in "kite building, multi-line competition, aerial photography, and more." There are many more kite groups on the Web besides the AKA, including groups in Molokai, Hawaii; Berkeley, California; Kitty Hawk, North Carolina; and all points in between. I must tell you, I was stunned.

If nothing else, the styles and sizes of kites will amaze you. There are winged box, dual line, quad line, sport style, round, angular, vipers, cobras—even kites shaped like eagles, hula girls, clowns, and, my personal favorite, a beautifully colored rainbow of a kite called the Peter Pan Boat Kite. And it flies.

There are conventions, associations, exhibitions, and demonstrations of various kinds of kites. Unless you are already a kite aficionado, you'll be amazed at the selections, shapes, and colors that abound in the kite world.

There are videos for sale to teach you how to fly for fun and for competition. I would have to say that the "funnest" (my wife's word) looking way to fly a kite is with the kite buggy. It looks like an overgrown kid's toy (for an overgrown kid?) with three wheels, but no pedals or steering wheel. The tires are fat to help when rolling across a variety of terrains. The basic premise is to get your kite into the air and then plop down onto the seat of your buggy. You steer the buggy by directing your kite with the wind and you turn or do tricks by directing the kite as you wish. You make your own speed limit—and

Go Build a Kite!

If you decide that you'd rather build than buy a kite, here's where you need to go: www. aka.kite.org. This is the Web site for the American Kitefliers Association. If you want info about kites, you'll find it here. Good luck!

brakes—based on how good you are at kite flying. This I would like to try.

However, you might decide to stick to regular kite flying with your child, because only one of you can ride in the buggy. (After all, this book is about spending time with your child, not about activities that will make them yell, "When's it going to be my turn, Dad?!") A day of kite flying at the park is great, but why not take it to the max and try some competition flying? I found literature online that showed diagrams of some of the sequences you'd have to master in a kite-flying competition, such as infinity, ladder down, the jump, the mount, the pyramid, and many, many more. (Of course, most of these look as if they would be impossible to master—for me anyway.) Some of the competitions can get pretty serious, not unlike the Indy 500. Kite fliers have pilots (drivers) and launch crews (pit crews) and every variety of official to make sure the competition is fair.

I must add a word of caution here. I can see some dads getting a bit overzealous and competitive with this activity. Remember—the point is to have *fun* with your child. Let your child pull the string sometimes.

One last thought. Many kite "dealerships" also sell a variety of kite-related items, up to and including hang gliders. In my Web search, I came across a site advertising hang gliders and it brought to mind a family memory from several years back. We had taken a driving trip through a series of campgrounds around Northern California. We had just come from Sequoia National Park and we pulled into a place called Dunlap. It wasn't even large enough to get its own population sign, but it did have a large eatery with two small cabins in the rear. Did I say cabins? I meant old wooden frames under a loose tar roof, outdoor plumbing—but with cable TV. I made the mistake of renting these facilities for the evening, and though that was at least ten years ago, I can still feel my family's icy stares on that warm summer night. They hated it, but I like to think of it more as a place that served a decent meatloaf sandwich—along with the worst night's stay in America. The highlight of that interlude, however, was the huge sign over the restaurant on the afternoon of our arrival. A banner hung across the length of the roof and, I swear we have a picture of it someplace, read: HANG GLIDERS' CONVENTION! On a smaller sign, just underneath, it read: WELCOME ARCHERS.

I ask you, are those two groups compatible . . . or is one group there at the other's expense?

Now's the time. Grab your kid and go fly a kite!

47

All Aboard!

Here's an activity that literally plans itself: Take your kids for a train ride.

There's just something enchanting about riding a train. Whether you're on a trip from Boston's North Station to Grand Central Station in New York, from O'Hare International to downtown Chicago, or traveling along the Pacific Coast Highway from L.A. to Monterey, there's nothing like taking a train trip. There is absolutely no other mode of travel that feels the same or is as much fun.

Years ago when we lived in L.A., I piled the kids into the car, drove downtown to Union Station, and our adventure began. Many stations still have grand buildings constructed in the heyday of the rail system. The ones I've visited are still architectural visions to behold. Many have high, high ceilings with murals representing historical events of the railroad or the area, intricately laid marble floors, hand-carved, roll-back wooden benches where movie stars, presidents, kings, and commoners have sat over the years.

Once ticketed and out on the concourse, my children's eyes nearly popped as they saw row upon row of trains, all ready to depart to intriguing locales. (I would think that the HARRY POTTER book series has been a boost for young readers wanting to travel by train. If you haven't yet read the books or seen the movie, this would be a great way to start your adventure with your children. I was totally captivated by the characters and read the entire series one book right after the another. A readers' note here: I wouldn't waste my time searching for platform 9¾ when you arrive at your station.)

We boarded our train for a trip down the coast to Santa Fe Depot in San Diego. It was fun to watch as the kids sat down and looked around at the unfamiliar setting. We have traveled a lot, sometimes by car, but mostly by airplane. I was curious about what they were thinking and looking for, so I asked. We had already begun to pull out of the station and one of my children nervously asked, "When do they show you the stuff about seat belts and barf bags?" It was fun to let them discover that, unlike most other types of travel, this was one where you could get up and walk around—particularly to the club car for pizza, soft drinks, ice cream, cookies, and, well, you know the drill. On a train, *everyone* gets to relax and enjoy the scenery, something only the passengers get to do in a car, and only those with window seats get to do on a plane. A train trip can be an activity that you can do as a day trip, a whole weekend, or even over an extended vacation.

I have such fond memories of train trips. I remember as a boy traveling with my dad from Louisiana to Arkansas to visit

Next Stop . . .

If you don't have the time to allow for a train ride, how about a walking tour of the station itself? There's history in most every building, no matter the age, and there's usually someone who remembers "way back when."

Ask to see any old relics, photos, mementos, vintage train cars, whatever. Show an interest, and they'll show you a great time.

one of our distant relatives. It would be years later before my next train ride. That one came courtesy of the U.S. Navy. I was inducted in New Orleans and boarded the *Sunset Limited* heading for Charleston, South Carolina, for further assignment. Truly alone for the first time in my "not quite an adult yet" life, I wandered the train proudly wearing my Navy blues and found myself in the car at the end of the train, a rather ornate club car that offered a panoramic view. The car was crowded, so I sat on one of the sofa-like seats, watching the sun go down and the Big Easy start to slip away as we began to roll the twenty-nine miles across Lake Pontchartrain. I looked across the car at three nuns sipping their drinks. Two of them seemed much older than the third one. It seemed, from the younger nun's very animated chatter, that she had never seen this part of the world before, nor much else for that matter. She also appeared not to have much resistance to the beverage(s) she was drinking. In other words, she was talking loud and acting as though she was schnockered. Up until that moment I had been feeling sorry for myself, having just said good-bye to everyone I'd known all my eighteen years. But I began to feel a little better now that I had entertainment in the form of the novice and, dare I say it, kinda cute, nun. The highlight for me and the shocker for the other two nuns—I could tell by their wide-eyed, drop-jawed expression—was when this real-live, non-musical version of Maria from *The Sound of Music* pushed her face against the window and started banging her finger against the glass to point out what she saw. As the train crossed the huge expanse of lake, she shouted at the top of her lungs, "Holy sisters in Christ, look at all that water!"

I chuckled all the way to Charleston. (I'm sure she was doing anything but chuckling when she woke up the next morning.)

Take your children on a train ride. You never know what adventure might await you.

48

I Pledge Allegiance

There's nothing as marvelous and inspiring as seeing Old Glory rippling in the breeze. Following the tragedy of September 11, 2001, it filled my heart with pride to see the American flag being flown in so many places where it hadn't been before. We live on a corner lot and decided to hang a flag from our roof so that people could see it from all directions. We even hung lights for the flag so that it could fly 24/7. Unfortunately, winds often knocked it from its perch—and it made me feel heartsick to find our flag, wounded, lying on the ground. We finally decided to attach it permanently to our garage door, where it would be better protected but could still be seen by all passing by.

Teaching your children about the American flag and its history can be a wonderful activity. At the same time, you instill patriotism, honor, and the importance of coming together when times are rough.

For instance, do you know why the Continental Congress selected the colors red, white, and blue? Give up? Well, I don't know, either. There is no definitive answer. However, in 1782, the Congress of the Confederation officially elected those colors for the flag with this interpretation: Red is for valor and hardiness; white stands for purity and innocence; and blue is for vigilance, perseverance, and justice. Legend has it that George Washington identified the choice of colors this way: The blue came from the skies, the red from our British heritage, and the white signified our secession and independence. But, actually, there is no *official* designation or meaning for the colors of the flag.

Another legend about the flag concerns Betsy Ross. How did a little-known seamstress get this all-important job over everyone else? It is told that she attended the same church as George Washington and often prayed in the pew next to his. Ah, networking at its finest.

Why is the flag sometimes referred to as "Old Glory"? A shipbuilder, Captain William Driver of Massachusetts, was so impressed with the majesty and soul of the flag that he coined the name as he unfurled it on one of his ships. He kept that same flag protected throughout the Civil War, not flying it again until it was placed over the Tennessee Capitol building, and the nickname spread, eventually becoming synonymous with the flag.

Here's another idea: We decided a long time ago to make a family flag together and display it at family gatherings. This is such an easy and fun project—the hardest part is knowing when to stop. First call a family meeting around the dining table. Have at the ready paper, colored pens, fabric scraps, fabric glue, and any other materials you might decide on as the project begins to take form. The first decision to make is: What will the family crest be? We often use the "Disney method" for decision making in family activities like this. It is said that whenever the Disney folks are tossing around ideas for new projects, the only rules are: There are no rules and there is no such thing as a bad idea. This means that any idea, no matter how foolish or outlandish it may sound, is still given serious discussion until the matter is settled. This may take longer than you expect it will, especially if you have really young children, but just relax and go with the flow. It *will* all come together at some point, and if you've read the chapter about creating games, you'll see that the free-flow dialogue can actually be rather fun—and funny. Remember, this is not a board meeting (or a "bored" meeting); this is time with the most important people in your life, your children.

Once you have decided on the crest, have your children design a symbol or character that personifies their pride in themselves. Now here's a chance for you to spend time one on one with each child and discover things you never knew about him or her—teaching the teacher, so to speak. Let them be as creative and demonstrative as they choose to be. We have one son whose artwork we can easily recognize. For example, at one elementary school parent/teacher night, teachers asked each set of parents if they could guess which artwork their child had produced. The assignment was to tear paper into ice cream cone shapes (does this fit our family or what?). With one quick glance, my wife and I, independently of the other, pointed to

Thirteen Folds

I received a touching e-mail message from a friend some time ago, which added to the explanation of why we take down the American flag the way we do in thirteen precise folds. Most of us know that the thirteen folds represent the original thirteen colonies, but I like these addenda:

The first fold of the flag is a symbol of living our lives with pride and honor.

The second fold is a symbol of our belief in eternal life.

The third fold is in honor and remembrance of our veterans who gave their lives defending our country.

The fourth fold represents our weaker nature and dependence on our creator in times of peace and war.

The fifth fold is a tribute to our country; may it always use our might to defend the right.

The sixth fold represents our hearts as we pledge allegiance to our flag, with liberty and justice for all.

The seventh fold is a tribute to our armed forces who protect our country and flag against all enemies, whether they be found within or without the boundaries of our republic.

The eighth fold is a tribute to mothers everywhere who are brave enough to send off their sons and daughters to defend our country.

The ninth fold is a tribute to womanhood, for it's through this divine nature of faith, love, loyalty, and devotion that the character of men and women who have made this country great have been molded.

the same spot on the far wall, to a picture of cones that exploded off the single page that the other kids had confined themselves to, and went at least twelve more scoops skyward,

Thirteen Folds (continued)

The tenth fold is a tribute to the father, for he, too, has given his sons and daughters for the defense of our country since they were first born.

The eleventh fold, in the eyes of a Hebrew citizen, represents the lower portion of the seal of King David and King Solomon, and glorifies in their eyes, the God of Abraham, Isaac, and Jacob.

The twelfth fold, in the eyes of a Christian citizen, represents an emblem of eternity and glorifies, in their eyes, God the Father, the Son, and the Holy Spirit.

And then we come to the thirteenth and final fold. As you complete this fold, showing your children the proper way to take down and present an American flag, you'll notice that what is shown now is a field of stars, reminding us of our nation's motto, "In God We Trust." And lastly, look at the shape of the folded flag. The triangular shape takes on the appearance of a military hat of long ago, reminding us of the lives that have been given so that we may have the freedoms we enjoy today.

Teach your children about our flag. Let them know the price that those who have gone before them paid. Let them know that life's not just about video games, television, and "things." Some of the greatest things in life aren't really things at all.

up to the classroom ceiling. It was incredible. Let your kids have creative freedom and you'll be amazed, surprised, and either puzzled or enchanted by what you'll see.

Choosing the background for the flag, the display pole, and so on will go quickly, but the real fun comes with the flag dedication ceremony. Plan a morning that the whole family can dedicate to preparing for this momentous event. If your video camera has the option of remote-control operation, read that chapter in the manual so you can finally use it. If not, this would be a chance to ask a neighbor (you know, that stranger you've been living next to for lo these many years?) to help out. Call your brother, sister-in-law, parents, cousins—get a crowd together, mostly for the extra thrill that this will generate for the kids.

I'm serious about this next idea. Call the local TV stations and newspaper(s). If it's a slow day and you present the idea appropriately, they might come out and use it as their "And finally . . ." type of story, or they might run a picture in the paper. Wouldn't that create a lifelong memory for your children? And won't you be proud when, as a grandparent (it will happen you know!), you're asked to come over to your now-grown child's house as he or she dedicates a family flag and you all look at clippings or videos of "way back then"? You might even consider adding members to the original flag as each child marries and has children, and then have a family get-together each summer, raising the flag when everyone arrives and leaving it up until the last one has departed.

The ceremony can be as grandiose as you're willing to make it, a special family tune playing through outdoor speakers as your own personal anthem. A podium or a music stand could be used for the patriarch (that's you) to give a short talk about family and family values. Family pictures around the family flag are priceless. Do it—it's fun and much easier than you might think.

49

Hoe! Hoe! Hoe!

In chapter 42, we talked about genealogy and the opportunity to find your roots. Here's an activity that helps you plant some new ones. It's a chance to break a little sweat with your kids and get some great rewards in the process. Why not take a little space at your "ranch" and grow a few things for the dining table? We have a swing set that the kids have outgrown that's taking up some valuable gardening space. I've been meaning to take it down for some time and hopefully will next week. If this is your first garden, chances are your crops will be bountiful—especially if you plant zucchini. Then you can share with the neighbors or let the kids set up a little produce stand on the corner. We always enjoy it when our neighbor brings us fresh tomatoes, beans, and squash.

The best way to begin is with a family meeting at—where else?—the dining table. Find out what each family member wants to grow and what is required for that plant to prosper. The children should be in charge of the meeting, taking notes and making a rough drawing of what the final garden will look like and where each item will be planted. Costs need to be figured in, with each child contributing some money to the project. This will give them a sense of ownership, which translates into a willingness to work on and maintain the garden—not to mention a sense of pride.

Next stop, your local garden center or nursery. The experts there will help you with information about fertilizers, nutrients, water management, and so forth. They can also tell you what tools you need to till your garden—specifically whether you can do it with hand tools or if you need to rent a gas-powered tiller. The same goes for planting. If you plan to mix in fruit trees, you need to determine the best place for sunlight, elevation, and watering needs. Be sure to ask what vegetables and fruits can and can't be planted together due to varying water needs.

The five basic steps for planting a garden, small or large, are:

1. Preparing the soil

2. Planting

3. Cultivating

4. Harvesting

5. Wolfing down the goodies you spent all that time and effort on

Two optional gardening methods are organic and hydroponics. Organic gardening means that rather than spreading synthetic fertilizers, you spread manure around (not to be confused with my news anchoring days, of course).

With hydroponics you grow food plants in a greenhouse setting or on a sunny windowsill. Rather than using soil, this type of planting is done in water, or in sand or gravel covered with water. Your plantings get the needed nutrients from chemicals you add to the water, rather than from the soil.

You can also use raised beds for planting. My wife prefers this type of gardening because, in her words, "It looks neater," and it saves a lot of wear and tear on your back. It also lets the kids get in a little hammering and nailing time constructing it, which might make the gardening idea a little more appealing to some children.

Don't let the fact that you live in an apartment keep you out of the dirt. Make a garden in a redwood planter, on a windowsill, or plant a few things in pots that you can place around the patio.

One vivid memory I have of gardening is of a huge field of cantaloupes growing across the road from my Uncle Phoenix's house near Converse, Louisiana. These nicely tanned and lined cantaloupes, just scarcely clinging to their life vines, seemed to be calling out to me. And I, being the charitable soul that I was, rescued those poor cantaloupes one by one. There is nothing better than sitting under a big old shade tree on a hot summer afternoon with a fresh, warm, "borrowed" melon, torn apart by eager hands, selfishly smooshing it into your face as you taste its sweet, juicy, perfectly ripened orange flesh. Forty-plus years can't dim that memory—or the taste or smell.

As you plan out your garden with your kids, plant a few cantaloupes for me and mine, because I'm still not really positive just when "next week" is coming around for the old swing set.

Easy-to-Grow Favorites

Fast sprouters: radishes, sunflowers, beans, squash, cucumbers

Early spring choices: peas, lettuce, carrots, spinach, melons, beans, pumpkins, herbs, corn

Summer choices: cucumbers, tomatoes, beans, summer squash, zucchini, broccoli, beets

50

Bubble, Bubble, Toil and Trouble

Boy did this one come out of left field! Here's an activity that you might not want to try, but trust me, it's a good one. As a matter of fact, I immediately sat down to write this after having done what I'm about to share with you.

The activity is . . . washing dishes. Yep, that is not a typo. I just finished helping my youngest son wash the dishes after a huge family dinner. In our family of four children, each child is assigned to wash dishes one week and clean the dining table another week, then he or she gets two weeks off. There are, of course, other chores such as cleaning their rooms, alternating trash carryout, and so on. But doing the dishes is the toughest job in their minds. The dish-duty changeover falls on Sunday and the mad scramble over whose job it becomes—even though we have it written out on the calendar each month—is inevitable.

I didn't realize until tonight that doing the dishes was a "moment machine" in and of itself. Generally, I help the new washer on Sundays because I actually enjoy it. I guess it kind of takes me back to a time when my brother and I did the dishes together until we grew up and moved out on our own, only to continue washing dishes until the children got old enough to fight about it.

As my son and I worked, I rinsed the dishes while he loaded the dishwasher (which, of course, we didn't have when my brother and I were growing up). My wife had prepared a special tangerine chicken dish (delicious!) using my old iron skillet. I turned to my son and told him how I'd had the skillet longer than I'd had him. He looked at me, surprised, and I told him the story: I bought the skillet when I lived in Boston and worked for CBS. My boss had overheard me talking about my fantastic chili and had asked me to make some. When I told him that I couldn't find my "fixin' pots," he purchased the skillet and a huge cast iron Dutch oven, and the party was on. The only prerequisite, as per my boss, was that I make the chili spicy hot. Having moved to Boston from Houston, Texas, I certainly knew how to make hot chili. Later that evening, after everyone had tried the chili, I approached my boss to ask how I'd done. He was standing in the open doorway, cold air pouring inside as snow fell in buckets outside. He gave me a thumb's up as he wiped the perspiration off his brow. I guess I earned my skillet and pot *that* night.

Next I asked my son if he knew how to clean the skillet and he gave me a "Duh!" look, indicating the dishwasher. I immediately warned him that he might not live to see his next birthday if he attempted to clean it thusly . . . and off I went on a discussion of how to season a skillet. I showed him how to

Good, Clean Fun

Any chore can be fun—it's all in how you approach the job. We had house cleaners for a while, but Joni and I decided the kids needed the experience. We made up a complete list of every housekeeping chore and divided it by four (the tougher jobs being done by the older kids).

Each week, at an assigned day and time, we'd hit the chores, running against the clock, and if we successfully finished before the designated time, we'd head out for ice cream and pizza. The first few times, we didn't make the deadline and the ones who did grumbled at those who didn't. Soon, they all realized that by pulling together and helping or by encouraging each other to hustle, the treats were attainable. This is a great method to teach teamwork!

wash it (a sin to many purists, I know), how to hand dry it, then how to really dry it over a fire (we use a gas stove), watching carefully as the wet spots disappear from the blackened iron. And then the final step: oiling down the pan to get it ready for the next usage. I could tell he was actually impressed, and knowing him, he'll be cooking something in the skillet soon, just to use his newfound knowledge.

I told my son about the time his uncle and I were about his age and we were goofing around with the glass water jug that we kept in the refrigerator. From time to time, Mom had us wash it before we refilled it. This particular evening, my brother was the washer, the coveted job, because he'd finish first while I, the dryer, was left holding a wet rag, wet dishes, and enough water on the counters to float a toy boat. I had taken a break to get the water jug out of the fridge and decided to chug the last drops before handing it over to my brother for washing. Being the impatient guy that he was—and this being the last item to wash—he kept barking at me to hand it over, and finally tried to take it from me as I struggled to drink from the mouth of the jug. He let go—suddenly—causing the glass bottle's lip to hit my lip, chipping my front tooth in the process. I don't think we ever told our parents just how my tooth got chipped—until now. Sorry, Mom. (Maybe this is also the time to tell about the time my brother threw a fork at me and how it stuck in the top of my bare left foot. On second thought, maybe not.)

I shared some more stories with my son as we finished the dishes, taking longer than usual because of the wonderful conversations we shared. I dare you! Offer to take over the dishwashing chore one evening—with your child as your helper—and you'll see what a memorable time you can have.

51

Do You Believe in Rainbows?

And so, we end as we began, talking about time. There are literally thousands of other ideas that I could have included in these pages. But *what* you do is so much less important than *that* you do. Don't be afraid to spend time, one on one, with your children. You can learn so much, about them . . . and about yourself. If you've read this book and tried just one of the ideas I've given you, you know what I'm talking about. If you haven't tried yet, then you have no clue.

I exhort you at least to try. What you do today will—and I can't emphasize that one word, *will*, enough—make a difference. It really is up to you. If you don't start the ball rolling, who will? Your dad's dad was a standoffish kind of guy, so was your dad, and so are you. Guess what? Your children will be that way with their children, and so on, unless *you* change things now.

How tough is it? Pick an activity and try it, just once, and I'll give you double your hugs and happiness back if you're not 100 percent satisfied (but you will be—guaranteed!).

Sometimes it's hard to let go of the hurt that prevents you from being the daddy that you always wanted. Sit down, alone, and run that through your mind for a while. Then realize that's the legacy that you're giving your children. It's time to stop the "pity party" and own up to your responsibilities. Go give them a hug, and a kiss, and tell them that you love them. And then go get a cheeseburger together.

I try my best every day to be a good and loving father. Do I succeed? *No*, not every time. I get busy, selfish, and preoccupied, too. But I try. I've got four young minds and hearts who, one day, will be going through all the ups and downs, heartaches and happiness that you and I have gone through. I want to make sure that they've got a proper map to follow. Every one of us could just roll over and pull a blanket over our heads because our childhood wasn't the greatest, but here's your chance to make it all better. Be the "he" who you wanted to see!

Worship with your children. I could preach to you here and tell you how you should come to my church (and you should), but you have the freedom to choose to worship as you choose. Just make sure that you choose. So many adults say, "Oh, I'll just let Junior choose when he is older. I don't want to force religion on him." That's a copout. That's not what they need. They need guidance, they need advice, they need leadership. They need your time.

So you want to do this, but . . . tomorrow. I understand. What's one more day?

As a young man, I moved to Hawaii for work. I went first to the big island of Hawaii, to the town of Hilo, to help run a startup radio station with the on-air promo "Hello, Hilo!" We thought we were cool, but not many others did. I left there to work as a television news reporter for the NBC affiliate in Honolulu on the island of Oahu. After living in an apartment with a partial view of Diamond Head that slowly disappeared each day with the progressive construction of a high-rise just outside my patio, I moved to the other side of the island. I found a tiny, beat-up one-bedroom house up on a hillside just off of the Kamehameha highway, outside of the village of Kaneohe. The drive in to work was terrific, over the Nuuanu Pali ("pali" means cliff in Hawaiian) and then down into Honolulu. Coming over the pass was great, the city and the ocean laid out before me. But going back to my little grass shack, peaking the Pali pass, with a view of the less-traveled way of Kaneohe Bay was absolutely breathtaking. I marveled at the flowers, trees, and bushes, thinking that everything here was ten times larger, more beautiful, and richer looking than I had ever seen before. Hibiscus plants with flowers large enough to wear as a hat grew everywhere. Birds-of-paradise plants that I'd only seen pictures of before were so thick in some places that they actually needed thinning, but I just didn't have the heart to do it.

As I took in the delicious smells and unbelievable views each day, I remembered how my father loved to work in the yard. Several times in this book, I've written about my father—the frogs, his famous burgers, and bowling. Although I had moments with him, I never spent a lot of time with him. I never really got to know him. After my childhood had passed us both by and I moved on, I kind of left him behind. I remember the day I left for the Navy, telling my parents good-bye at the airport. My father got teary-eyed, yet he never reached out to me.

They left me at the curb, and I watched him stare straight ahead as they drove away, wondering how he could cry about my departure but not get any closer to me than that. I guess maybe he was afraid, but it still cut like a knife.

We stayed in touch, and then a few years later, when I was living in paradise, I thought of him. I was too broke to call home, so I wrote to him about the beauty of this place. He began to write me back, and the closeness that I had always wanted as a child began to develop, on paper. I told him that I was saving my money so that I could buy a ticket to fly him over to spend some time with me and witness how nature had done so easily what he had spent most of his life trying to do. He wrote me back to let me know that he would come . . . one day . . . just not right now. Every letter ended the same way: some day, not now.

The phone jolted me awake one morning around 3:00. I reached over in my sleepy haze and grabbed the screaming instrument, but couldn't make out what was being morosely conveyed. As I slowly came to my senses, the words finally began to sink in. It was my brother calling, telling me, "Bob, Dad died."

I don't remember how I responded, or even if I did. All I remember is sitting at the rickety dining table next to the oversized front window, staring out into the darkness, feeling such a heavy emptiness inside me. As the sun began to reach across the ocean, I stared out through hurting, cried-out eyes, angry at my father for not keeping his promise to come see me. Spread before me, as God perfectly lighted the diorama below, I saw tethered boats floating in a bay so crystal clear they appeared to be drifting in the air. In the distance, as the two-lane road twisted to the right, making its way around the mountain, I stared at the lush, majestic, emerald green walls. Many mornings before going to work, I had stood at this very spot, looking out at this perfect scene. This morning, filled with the sorrow that I'd never be able to share this view with my father as I had planned, the clouds begin to shift and move as if to frame a painting. And then the most perfectly formed, bright rainbow appeared, wrapping itself around the mountain, one end behind it, the other dipping into the smooth, aqua waters of Kaneohe Bay. I stared at the rainbow, captivated, having never seen anything like this in all the mornings before.

On the flight back to the mainland that night, after having sold or given away everything I owned to buy the ticket, I couldn't sleep. As I tossed in the small airplane seat, my mind wouldn't let go of what had happened that morning. I pulled out a piece of scrap paper and began to write about it. I wrote about how, as I stared at that incredible rainbow, filled with fury and despair, I trembled as I heard, more clearly than I had heard anything in my life, the voice of my father telling me, "I told you that I would come." All at once, I felt at peace with the knowledge that he *did* love me. He loved me enough to keep his word, even in death.

It's been more than thirty years since my father passed away, but the memory is as strong as if it had happened this morning. I still cry like a baby as I retell this story.

Don't let another second pass before you grab your children, tell them how much you love them . . . and spend some precious time with them. Do it while you still have the time to give.

Show them a rainbow. Believe in rainbows. I still do.

Fast and Furious: 52 Quick Ideas

So you've been through all the ideas in every chapter—and still want more? Even if you've only tried a few of the ideas in the rest of the book, here are fifty-two more ideas for fun, easy, rewarding activities to do with your children.

1. Make an Emergency Kit

Grab a kid and have him help you put together an emergency kit for the house. You can buy these kits ready made, of course, but that would defeat the purpose, now wouldn't it? Take a look at what the readymade kits offer and decide how much of that you'd like to replicate. Don't forget a kit for the trunk of the car, too. Be sure to include nonperishable food, warm clothes and/or blankets, tools, first-aid supplies, flares, and a small amount of cash.

Once you and your child have made the kits you might want to plan a day of "emergency reaction drills," mapping out escape routes, learning how to treat minor wounds, and other basic first-aid and disaster-recovery methods. It's a great one-on-one activity—and could come in handy in an emergency.

2. Head to the Hardware Store

Is there a man out there who doesn't like—okay, *love*—going to the hardware store? Walking the aisles and looking at all that remodeling stuff offers the same thrill that a woman gets window shopping at Victoria's Secret. (Too bad the reverse, men at Victoria's Secret/women at the hardware store, isn't equal. Okay, okay, I guess it is for the men.) Although *everything* in a hardware store looks great to us, you probably can't say the same for your children. So, take your child with you and ask her to do what might seem, to you, impossible: Find among the sacred merchandise what she considers to be some truly goofy items. (Remember, this has nothing to do with our egos, this is all about them.)

Then, take the items they select (as long as they're inexpensive) and do something fun with them. For example, say your child selects some strands of colored wire. You will *not* be using the wire to do what you'd normally do with it. Instead, you and your child will bend the wires into funny characters. (You must not shed tears during this activity!) You could also make a checkers set using nuts and bolts or fashion a playhouse out of PVC pipe.

3. Camp Out in the Backyard

For the "littler" ones, have a campout in the backyard. Watch the stars, sing around a make-believe campfire, make s'mores the easy way (in the microwave), then bring them outside. And don't forget the bug repellant!

A warning here. Make sure you bring along plenty of light. Kids panic at the sounds of the wild (even if it's just your cat approaching the tent), so be prepared to comfort and console them . . . until about thirty minutes after dark. That's when things get better—because that's when they decide that their beds are where they would really rather be. And the campout ends.

4. Make a Chalk Walk

The next time you're doing yard work, turn the mower off and grab some chalk. Think fun. Here's a chance to try your artsy side with your child. Turn your sidewalk into a chalk walk.

Spend the afternoon helping your child draw hopscotches, landscapes, riddles, and funny faces. After a few tries, you might even get good enough to create some really special-looking sidewalk panels.

Check your local newspaper for your city's community art listings (usually in the Saturday paper). From time to time, you'll find chalk art festivals at neighborhood public parks. To take it one step farther—and better—you and your child could even plan a chalk art festival for your own neighborhood. Have your child make a list of his friends, then invite them and their parents for the "First Annual Dad and Kid Sidewalk Chalk Art Show!" Be sure to have the other parents and children bring—and help serve—refreshments!

5. Make a Nature Journal

Wherever you live, there are critters and plants, and depending on your kid's interests, you can make it a project to watch spiders, fruit trees, or wild flowers by the roadside.

Pick a spot you know your child would enjoy: the river, the desert, the valley, anywhere that would make a fun day trip. Grab some burgers, fries, and a shake, or pack a picnic lunch, and head to the hills. Make sure you have a few art supplies (paper, colored pencils, stickers, and so on) so that as the inspiration hits, you and your child can sketch, draw, or scribble to your heart's content. You will be amazed at the creativity that will pop out of not just your child but you . . . if you let the kid in you come out to play. At the end of the day, head over to the local print shop and have them laminate your drawings and bind them. This makes a great gift for Mom (and gives beaucoup brownie points for Dad) and your child will enjoy it all, too.

6. Refinish a Piece of Furniture

There are videos and TV shows that take you from the basics all the way through to the finished product. If you don't have any idea which grade of sandpaper to use or which varnish and stripper work best, don't worry. The many do-it-yourself shows, books, and tapes will make you look like an old pro. Your kids will never know that Pop *doesn't* know everything about everything.

The best way to find pieces to "practice" on before trying it on a family heirloom is to scout garage sales, thrift stores, or antique shops and rescue an old, beat-up piece that you can turn into a treasure—or at least, better-looking trash.

7. Build a Fort

Now that you're all messed up from the sanding and varnishing, you might as well add a little paint to the mix. Find a giant box—like the kind refrigerators and other large appliances come in—and turn it into a fort, a castle, or a store. If you can't find a large discarded box, go to a neighborhood box store and spend a few bucks on a wardrobe box. It will fill the bill nicely.

You know it's true that a child often loves the box the gift comes in as much as the gift . . . sometimes even more. So, here's a chance to give her the gift of a lifetime with hardly any expenditure at all. Find out if she would rather be a member of the U.S. Cavalry, a knight, or a princess—or perhaps a merchant at one of the stores where you shop. Once that's decided, sit down at the dining table and draw out your plan. Let your child tell you where to put the windows, turrets, doors, and so on. If you're lucky enough to find a couple of boxes—wow, a two-roomer. A little cutting, a little painting, and a lot of cheers for Dad from his little one.

8. Teach Them to Invest

Teach your child about the stock market. First, encourage your child to save enough of his allowance to become a mini Wall

Street wizard. Look for inexpensive stocks in companies your child will know—makers of movies, tennis shoes, computers, and so on. Teach him how to read the financial section of the newspaper to follow the market.

And then teach him about the "rule of 72." This will blow his little mind. Pick a CD (certificate of deposit), mutual fund, or whatever investment instrument you choose and find out the annual interest rate. Let's say it's 8 percent. Take the number 72 and divide it by the interest rate, 8 percent, and that will tell you how long it will take your investment to double. In this case, 72 divided by 8 equals 9, so in nine years, your child's money will double . . . and if left there, will continue to double every nine years. After your child's gaping mouth closes again, take him to see your financial planner (you do have one, don't you?) and show him how, through careful planning and dollar-cost averaging (investing a specified amount on a regular basis), when he hits retirement age, he could easily be a millionaire.

9. Make Dirt!

Kids get a kick out of seeing how nature really works, how organic products decompose, and how to reuse veggies and other green products you used to throw away. The way to do this is to make a compost pile. You'll find step-by-step construction plans on the Internet. (Choose a search engine, type in "compost pile," and bingo.)

Start after you've mowed the lawn. Pick up the leaves or grass clippings and then layer them in a large wooden container (it might take a whole weekend just to build this box), alternating with layers of dirt. Think of how many things you can add to the mix while teaching about recycling and nature (and think how your plants will love this rich soil!). Your kids will start saving orange peels, wilted lettuce, and countless other plant products to add to the mix. Every week or so, turn the compost to mix it.

10. Stage a Weather Prediction Contest

Teach your kids about the different kinds of clouds, what barometric pressure is, why the wind blows, and what humidity means. Jot down everyone's weather predictions for the upcoming week, and see who comes closest.

You can turn this into a geography lesson, too. As they learn about the weather, have them find the weather map in your daily newspaper. Most are printed in color and cover the entire country. Cut one weather map out of the paper and hang it on the wall in the child's room. The geography lesson comes in as you get your child to find Grandma's, or Uncle Ken's hometown, or the capitals of each state, and so on. Then, as they check their weather predictions, they can also check the weather conditions across the country. How hot is it in Washington, D.C., compared to Washington State? How about the highs and lows of Truth or Consequences, New Mexico? What a great way to teach your child something new—without her even knowing that she was being taught something.

11. Make a Swing

Any kind of swing. You remember the great tire swings, canvas strap swings, and wooden discs we used to play on? Help your child build one. If you don't live where this is possible, make it a game to search out the best parks with the best swings. If your child is old enough and strong enough to steady himself, push his swing, carefully of course, until he's going just high enough to achieve momentary weightlessness.

If your park has one of those tire swings that hang horizontally attached to a chain in three places, allowing it to spin freely, you're in for a real treat. As you spin your child in one direction he'll begin to get a little dizzy. Stop the spinning quickly and immediately spin a turn or two in the opposite direction—his dizziness will disappear instantly. Cool!

12. Curl Up with a Good Book

When was the last time you snuggled with your child in the kids' section of the local library? Stack up a dozen picture books and read them all.

The only caution here is that *all* kids love to hear stories read aloud. I did this once with one of my kids and discovered that first one, then two, then three, then a gathering horde of kids had surrounded us, drawn to their stories being brought to life by a voice. You will hear giggles and peals of laughter at things you might not consider funny at all. But it's infectious. Once you get into the characters, you'll have the kids howling in no time. You don't have to be a voice actor to do this. Just have a little love for your child and it will come naturally to you. Read the words on the pages out loud and their imaginations will do the rest.

13. Create a Rube Goldberg Contraption

Rube Goldberg was the guy who thought up those elaborate whizzing, dinging, plopping machines that take a ball or a marble through a virtual obstacle course of mechanical fun before it arrives at its destination. You can make a simplified version of one of these contraptions with your child. See if you can get a marble to roll through a cardboard tube, a metal pipe, a coiled wire, then have it drop onto a catapult, and so on. Some great "ingredients" are sections of PVC piping, funnels, mini basketball hoops, hamster wheels, and wire hangers bent into tracks for the marble. Tape or fasten everything together as best you can, and get your child thinking about physics. Some of the more elaborate contraptions ring bells, trigger lights or music, and last for several minutes before the ball arrives. If you have a large room, see if you can fill it with an intricate system of tracks and tubes. (For more info, see www.rube-goldberg.com.)

14. Smoosh Polaroids

For this one you'll need a Polaroid camera. Take some pictures, but don't wait for them to dry as the instructions recommend. Instead, press the surfaces with a Popsicle stick (or your fingernail) and you can move your facial features around. The results are hilarious—you can make super-wide noses, ultra-tall foreheads, and wild hair. Great fun and huge laughs. You can even go and get them enlarged at the local drugstore photo enlarger, and send them to friends (and what a Christmas card, eh?).

15. Make a Family Time Capsule

Boy, here's a fun way to get a kid to clean her room. While you were at the hardware store earlier, you picked up a metal tube, box, or other airtight container for this activity. The container should be about the size of a mailbox so that it can hold several items. Pick a few things for the capsule from each child and something from Mom and Dad. You might also include reminders of the pets, a picture of the cat, a hamster toy, or a chewed-up doggy bone.

If there are more items than you have room for, have the official deciders (your child and you) make the call about what goes in and what doesn't. Have your child then write herself a letter describing her life now . . . and predicting how life will be years from now when you plan to open the capsule. Be sure to include family photos.

Decide to wait at least ten years to dig up and open the capsule. Very important: Make sure you draw a map of where you plant the time capsule so that you can be sure you can find it. If you decide to change homes before the time is up, dig up the capsule, replant it at your new home, and add a few more years to the opening date if the time is nearly up.

One last thought. Before you seal the capsule, and without your child seeing, sneak in a love letter to them for a nice warm future surprise.

16. Go to the (Silent) Movies

Here's how you do it: Rent a corny movie and turn the sound off. (Actually, you can do this with many of the big-budget Hollyweird films coming out every week.) But it's best with the older films—and black and white is the best. You can assign your kids to "talk" for a certain character or they can just jump in whenever they want. Hilarious!

17. Whittle Away the Hours

Here's a lost art that deserves a comeback. In the Scouts program, kids earn their tote-and-chip award, meaning they can carry a Scout-approved knife with them on campouts and such. Teaching a child about handling knives is, of course, very important. Never pass a knife to another person blade first. If you open a knife, you close the knife. Strike the blade away from you and not toward you.

A great thing to start beginning "carvists" on is a bar of soap. This will teach them to be careful and gentle so that the carving doesn't break apart. The next step is to move up to soft wood. After a while, any wood will do. If there is a real interest in this, hobby shops have all kinds of paraphernalia to take this way beyond soap carving. Then again, I think it sounds pretty cool spending a lazy afternoon just whittling on the porch.

18. Plan an Archeological Dig

Set it up ahead of time, hiding interesting fossils, pieces of crystal, unusual rocks, shells—whatever your child would love to find. Use a small area of your backyard, a sand box, or even a shoebox filled with sand. This can easily be compared to an Easter egg hunt, but with fossilized eggs.

Grab one of your old hats and shirts and dress him up like Indiana Jones. Have him tell a story, detective style, about the "mystery" he is uncovering as he makes his discoveries.

19. Go to the Circus— Right at Home

Find a very grassy spot in the yard that the dog hasn't visited and drag out some lawn chairs, ribbons, rope, buckets, oranges, and so on. Learn stunts, juggling, acrobatics, clown paint— even teach your pets some tricks.

You can tumble with your children, paint their faces, and then let them paint yours. You must remember that much of their fun comes in seeing you having fun and taking part in their little play action. It might behoove you to stop by the bookstore before "circus day" and pick up a book on very simple juggling tricks. I'm *not* a juggler, but I stunned myself by following the "Klutz" instructions, watching as the three tennis balls made a few circles in the air without dropping to the ground. What a thrill that was for me. Try it and then teach your child. You will have as much fun as she will!

20. Take Your Kid to Work

Don't wait for the official "Bring Your Kid to Work" day. Take him in on a Saturday when he can relax and have the run of the place. You will both enjoy this much more than having to watch yourselves around your coworkers.

Make sure you visit the most important area at your work place: the break room with all the tempting machines. Make sure you also have a pocket full of change. Your child will love it.

21. Hop on the Bus, Gus

Here's one kids of all ages will enjoy. Ride your city's public transportation system to a cafe in another part of town, or to a museum or sports stadium you've never visited. There are subways, rail transportation, buses, and, in some cities, trolleys or cable cars.

If you wonder whether your child would enjoy this, consider those ads for San Francisco on TV (or think about the last time you visited that city). You've seen the world-famous cable cars. If you take your eyes off the beautiful scenery of this absolutely gorgeous city for a moment and concentrate on the cable-car riders, you'll notice that, for the most part, they are all smiling and laughing. It's because even the "big kids" love riding the cable cars—or buses, or subways. Take your little kids out for a day of adventure, sights, and, of course, an ice cream cone.

22. Go to a Free Show

Any kind of show or festival will do. Watch the upcoming events listings in your local newspaper for things like vintage auto shows, flower festivals, and other fun freebies.

I recently saw an ad for an auto museum that briefly mentioned America's Godfather of the sports car, Carol Shelby. Yes, *that* Shelby was going to make a brief appearance the next evening. I packed my three boys into the car and we had a blast checking out the various cars at the show and, at last, meeting "the man." He was there for a brief moment, signed a few pictures, and then, like Elvis, left the building.

Had Mr. Shelby not been there, we would have gone just to see the cars. It would have been worth it just to see my three boys talking, laughing, and generally getting along wonderfully with each other because of this common denominator. Check the papers. There's a whole lot going on out there.

23. Snow Sculpt

Instead of fashioning a mere snowman, really get into the art of snow sculpting. Make a dragon, a snow castle, or a cartoon character. (Hint: Start small.) Use food coloring and props to complete the effect. You can even sprinkle powdered gelatin to color your creations. Be sure to take pictures. Another fun idea is to establish a traditional competition among neighbors or friends. Get five or six entries in your "snow fest," and let passers-by judge the winner. The local newspaper might even run pictures!

If you happen to be one of those poor, unfortunate souls who live near a beach and aren't blessed with frozen temperatures and toes, you can do the same sculpting with sand . . . wearing a bathing suit.

24. Make a Clock, a Lamp, or a Music Box

These are all easy projects. You can buy the workings at the hardware store. You can turn any hollow container into a lamp with simple wiring; any flat object, such as a piece of tile, a computer disc, or an old record, can become a clock. You can buy the works for a music box and glue them into wooden boxes or tuck them into a favorite stuffed animal. Hardware stores and specialty shops can supply the inexpensive components, and your child will be so proud of her finished project. Be sure to stand back and let her do most of the work, with your supervision. These make great gifts, too!

25. Turn Your Kitchen into a Mad Scientist Lab

Get out mixing containers, ingredients, aprons, and even goggles if you wish. Let your kids mix harmless ingredients and experiment with colors, smells, and textures. Older kids could use chemicals from science supply stores. It's fun to see what gloppy stuff your kids create. Or try to put together an actual cake from interesting ingredients and bake it. See how it comes out.

You can also make clay, goop, or papier-mâché. You'll easily find recipes for these and more on the Net.

26. Tour the Fire Department

You might assume your kids do this in school, but they don't always. And a one-on-one tour is much better than a tour for thirty-six kids. Talk with the firefighters and have them tell your child more about their jobs. We all witnessed the heroic deeds of these wonderful men and women after the terrorist attacks on New York City and the Pentagon on September 11, 2001. But this is what these people face each and every day on their jobs. Every fire they head out to fight is a potentially perilous situation.

After your tour, the best thing you can do to help them and your child, is to then go home and practice what they preached. Use the experts' information and your child's curiosity to make your house fire safe. Have your child set up some fire drills, teaching the rest of the family the best escape routes. You say you wanted to be a fireman when you grew up, eh? Well, here's your chance.

27. Plan a Fancy Evening

This is a chance for you and your child to wear your most formal attire and show your best manners. At some point, at school, church, or a friend's party, your child is going to need to know proper etiquette. Here's your chance to get the "man's" side in on how this all works. Teach your boy how to respect the opposite sex. Teach him about opening doors and letting her through first, pulling back her chair, and walking on the street side as a measure of protection and a sign of respect. Make sure he knows that girls appreciate being treated well. Teach your girl to accept nothing less than respect and honorable treatment from boys. Tell her and show her that she is of infinite worth and reinforce that any boy who tries to treat her as anything less isn't worth being around. Teach boys and girls about dining manners, how to place their napkins in their laps (and use them!), which fork for which dish, how to be gracious about the food being served, and so on.

To make the evening extra special, take your little dude or dudette to a formal shop and spend a little dough for fancy outfits for them and for you. Add in tickets for a concert, opera, or play, and you are set for an evening to remember. This activity will take some preplanning—and presaving—but will be worth it for the lifelong memory it will provide. Don't forget to take photos.

28. Teach Them to Follow the Ropes

Teach your kids to read and follow directions. After all, how many times do we open that new stereo box and completely ignore the instruction sheet? Instead, next time you buy something that needs assembly or hookup, involve the kids. Build a shed together, set up a computer, install a dimmer switch, frame a photo. Lay out the instructions next to the parts and pieces. Carefully go over your inventory, making sure all of the parts are there. It is so frustrating to try to put something together when you have missing parts—especially if you can't figure out what's missing. Do your inventory first and this will solve that problem.

My older brother still asks me to put things together for him when I visit. This is a very valuable life skill for kids to have. We once bought an unassembled barbecue grill and, even though it took one of my sons and me a few months of Saturdays, we finally got it together. I'm not sure that all the pieces are in the right places, but it grills with the best of them. Letting your child be in charge of projects like this is great for building confidence, too.

29. Make a Tubular Telephone

Bendable plastic tubing is available at the hardware store for just a few cents a yard. Buy yards of it, then send your child into one room with one end, while you stay in, say, the family room with another end. Whisper and see if he can hear you. Experiment with how sound travels.

Try branching another off the first one. You could even take him on a trip back in time to when you did the old tin can/string phone trick. Secret tip: If you don't tell them that the tin can/string phone is an "old" idea, they may think it's the latest and coolest thing. It's worth a try.

30. Display a Collection

Together, make (or purchase) a display case, or mount the objects artistically in your child's bedroom. You could run a shelf around the walls up near the ceiling to display stuffed animals, train sets, dolls, or license plates. Butterflies, watch faces, jewelry, rocks, and stamps look great in a memory box. You could center on a wall an interesting display of baseball caps, snow globes, hubcaps, or other memorabilia.

One idea (that we stole from a friend who had stolen it from another friend) was to get some little picket-fence planter boxes, about six inches tall. We found them at a local nursery. I mounted them over the windows of my daughter's room and then she filled them with stuffed animals and other toys. It looks as if her playthings are having a party above her bed each evening.

I also collect canes and walking sticks. One of my sons decided he likes them also and now brings home various twisted twigs and sticks for his own collection. We made a crude—but pleasing to him—"stick stand" for his collection. He did the hammering and some of the cutting. It will never be on exhibit at the Louvre, but he likes it and I smile each time I see it, thinking of the fun we had making it.

31. Videotape Grandparents and Older Relatives

Have your child be the interviewer and ask about grandparents' and other relatives' good memories, what life was like when they were young, their hopes for the future as young people, and their advice to others. You and your child can come up with a list of prompts to keep the interviewees talking. As you plan this activity, set up the video camera on a tripod so it's taping you and your child. Later, as you shoot the "real" interview, you'll be able to include the past and the future in the frame together. Ask your child what they think their grandparents' answers will be about their childhood so many years ago. Find out what questions your child would like to ask. This might take some prompting from you, but as you build the question list, your child will get the feel of it and start to add his own questions.

The best part is to rehearse the questions enough that, in so doing, you teach your child to listen. The point here is that to be a good interviewer, you must first be a good listener. After your child has gotten the questions down, once he asks the first one, his grandparents' answers may actually lead him in a totally different direction than simply reading from a list of questions. This also allows him to hear what's being said, rather than waiting for the silence after each answer so he can jump to the next question.

32. See a Play

Teach kids early to support the arts, and to support their community. You might even consider letting your child get involved in a production as an actor, extra, or stagehand. Every theater group needs extra help, from painting scenery to sweeping up before and after each production.

One important part of your child's development is teaching her to give service to others. As she learns with fun activities like this, she will continue this volunteerism as an adult.

33. Have a Heroes Day

Many of today's athletes and rock stars make pretty poor role models, so help your child select someone truly great to research. If that person is still living, have your child write him or her a letter. Wouldn't it be wonderful to receive a response to treasure forever? Expose your kids to lots of real-life heroes who were noble, brave, and showed integrity and compassion.

Talk to friends at church or at work about who they think are real-life heroes. You may walk past them every day without even knowing it. Every Sunday, I used to say hello to an older gentleman who was very shy. One evening I was invited to a presentation about a World War II pilot who had done some spectacular and heroic things. When the honored person was introduced, I was flabbergasted. It was that very shy and meek little man whom I greeted every Sunday. Here was a man who, in the prime of his life, put himself on the line every day. On every mission he was shot at—and his aircraft took frequent hits—and yet he continued to fly and fight back, and in doing so, helped preserve our freedom. Find a real hero, not some billionaire sports junky who whines because he has an ingrown toenail. Teach your child what heroism is really about, and then help your child plan a celebration to honor that person.

34. Make Shadow Puppets

This is wonderful, old-time fun, and kids of all ages get into it as they try to make their hands look like dragons, dogs, even celebrities. All you need is a darkened room, a blank wall, and a bright desk light to cast shadows.

First, position the light to shine brightly on the wall, then experiment with the distance of your posed hands. Move them forward and back toward the light until you get sharp, well-defined shadows. Use one hand to make the antlers of a deer, while the other forms the mouth. Bend one knuckle up to allow light through to form an eye. Overlap hands to make a tarantula. You could even perform a skit using your favorites.

35. Stage a Safety Contest/Game Show

Make up a list of the things you want your kids to know to stay street smart, protected from molesters, and prepared for emergencies. You ask the questions and award points for every right answer. Points can be redeemed for a reward of your choosing. Some sample questions are: "What do you do if you're home alone and a stranger comes to the door?" Or, "If someone tells you to keep a secret from your dad, what do you say?" Or, "You're at your friend's house and he wants to show you his dad's cool rifle. What do you do?"

36. Make Paper Airplanes

Use your childhood skills to pass on this noble art—or borrow a library book on the subject. It's amazing how elaborate some paper airplanes can be. Some require cutting and gluing, weighting different sections with card stock, and so on. But you don't have to get elaborate to have fun. Just try the various folds you remember from your own childhood, and see who can get the best loop-de-loop, the farthest distance, or the highest flyer. Kids even enjoy coloring and naming their airplane. You can also try putting stickers on the nose of the plane to add a tiny bit of weight, and see what happens.

37. Make a Movie Highlight Tape

Everybody loves a good laugh, right? And we all have favorite scenes from movies that we talk about and rehash, laughing all over again. How about putting together a tape of favorite movie moments? When you rent a movie and have a scene that's so hilarious you rewind it to play it again, add it to a master tape. Then, one night, just plug in the "best clips" and enjoy. Our family loves certain scenes from *The Princess Bride*, *Young Frankenstein*, *Monty Python and the Holy Grail*, *Dr. Dolittle 2*, *Stuart Little*, *King Creole* (with Elvis), *Dirty Rotten Scoundrels*, and a zillion others. You'll find movie lines that touch a funny spot for everyone in your family.

38. Honor Our Veterans

Take a plate of cookies, a basket of flowers, or a poster-size Get Well card to some of the great folks at your local VA hospital. Visit the traveling Vietnam Memorial when it comes to your town. Talk about the original founding fathers and what they did to secure our freedoms. Examine each of our wars and the many veterans who went into service for our country. Don't wait for Veterans Day—make a special Honor Day of your own. Kids will enjoy creating a "Thank you, we remember you" gift for local service people. Let them decide whether it's a baked good or a poster, and spend time with them creating this heartfelt remembrance.

39. Hold a Bubble Gum Contest

Buy a whole bag of bubble gum and see who can blow the biggest bubble. Or try a few packs of different brands to see which ones "bubble" the best. Invite friends over and make it a bubble gum party. See who can make the biggest bubble, the loudest-popping bubble, the quickest bubble, the tiniest bubble. You're sure to get plenty of laughs with this activity. Be ready with baby oil to take popped gum out of eyebrows. And be ready for tired jaws later (which means quiet kids!).

40. Help Endangered Species

Research endangered species in your area and do something to help them. Your child may also get interested in, for example, a species from the rain forest or giant pandas. Support your child in discovering ways to make a real difference. Library resources, Web sites, and magazines are all sources of great information about animals we may not always have around to enjoy unless we each help out. Our family has enjoyed *Zoobooks* magazine, which provides a lot of information about how we can raise people's awareness about endangered species and keep them around longer. Consider holding a fund-raiser (a car wash, a bake sale), and put up posters about the event that explain where the money will go.

41. Name Hats

This activity is going to sound very quick and easy (and perhaps a bit odd)—until you try it. It's especially good if you have to make a long drive or take a flight where boredom might set in. This game can go on for hours. You simply take turns naming kinds of *hats*. That's right, hats. The first one who can't think of a different kind of hat is out. You'll be amazed at how many types of hats there are.

At some point, announce that the reason for the game and the drive is because you're going to a hat shop. I know this might sound even sillier, but hold on. Check in your town's yellow pages and you'll more than likely find such a place. It might be in the "funkier" part of town, but that will just add to the adventure. I found such a place and was amazed at the weird and funny selection the shop carried. One hat was shaped like a birthday cake, candles and all. Another was in the shape of the pope's hat, while another looked like a Viking warrior's headgear. The selection went on and on. The truly fun part was watching the kids laugh, run to the next hat, try it on, and make faces and gestures fitting the character they were playing. Make sure you take a camera along for the special "hat day" derby. Oh, yes, they had a derby hat, too.

42. Be Phantom Helpers

Think of a neighbor or acquaintance who needs something done and do it. The idea is to do it without being discovered. Does a widow need her lawn edged? Could you take in someone's garbage cans? Be creative—maybe it'll be a ring-the-bell-and-run delivery.

This activity is especially fun and fulfilling during the holidays. If you don't know of a particular family in need, check with your church or make a few calls to various charity organizations. They will give you information about the family, such as the number and ages of kids and their particular needs. The greatest part of this activity is that after all the research (make sure the kids have a leading hand in doing all of this), planning, gathering, and delivering, doing it anonymously will teach your children a great life lesson. They will learn how gratifying helping others can be—particularly when giving is done without causing embarrassment to the needy receiver. Knowing you've done a great thing that no one else will ever know about is also a fun secret to have with your children.

43. Paint a Mural

Use a wall of your garage. Why not? Garages are usually pretty bland, and you can liven one up with some splashy kid art. If your neighborhood restrictions permit it, paint the entire outside of your garage. Across our nation's farmland areas you quite often see sides of barns painted. Although I'm not suggesting you live in a barn, it might still look cool to have a huge American flag painted on the side of your garage. This would work really well if it turns out that your house needed painting anyway. Paint the garage mural, leave it there while you finish painting the rest of the house, and then, to the cheers of your neighbors, repaint the garage.

Inside the garage, you could paint the tool bench, with silhouettes of each tool painted where it goes. Or dedicate one wall as your "budding artist" palette. Get some trim at the lumber yard and nail it on the wall, creating a "frame" for your child's painting. Depending on the size of the framed area that you frame, if she creates a masterpiece and you sell your house, you could cut this out, patch the hole, and take your "Picasso" with you.

44. Measure Your Kids As They Grow

Establish a place for measuring your kids as they grow. It can be a wall, a doorjamb, or a movable strip you can hang anywhere. Just be sure to mark their progress. Kids love craning their necks upward to see if they're catching up to you!

This is a tough one to leave if you move. You can take a painting from the garage, but most people use doorjambs to make their kids heights, and these are a little tougher to move. We're in that kind of a pickle now. One way to rectify this dilemma is to get a tall board and temporarily mount it beside your height chart. Have the children come out and have each one help reproduce the years of their growth on the new board. At the conclusion of the "remarking" ceremony, have each child stand against the board for the newest mark, officially making this new board the designated height chart that you will move to your new digs. Once at the new home, have a full-fledged dedication ceremony with music as well as funny and brief speeches, followed by treats, of course. It will be a fun day.

45. Stage a Water Wars Party

Invite your kids' friends and tell them to bring any kind of super soaker/water projectile/shooter they wish. Have a supply of water balloons handy, too. The idea is to get completely drenched (but not before drenching everybody else). This is perfect for hot summers, and clean, cheap fun.

In addition to everyone bringing their own soakers, make sure they bring a towel or two as your supply will quickly get "soaked up."

Note: Some of the kids will probably bring the latest super-mega-death blaster types of water assault guns, but not everyone will be lucky enough to have one. So, every twenty minutes or so, have everyone exchange water guns with the closest person (usually the one they've been blasting away at). This makes for a more fair and fun afternoon.

46. Make Ice Cream

If you've never made old-fashioned, hand-cranked, homemade ice cream, you are missing one of the great treats in life. Involve your kids in making this masterpiece come together. You can find hand-cranked ice cream makers at many hardware stores, and most come with recipes. I remember as a kid watching my dear Aunt Alice pluck fresh peaches off her tree, chop them up, then plop them in the mix. Delicious! Part of the taste expectation comes from all of the preparation. Most of the ice cream makers available today are electric, but if you can find one of the old hand-cranked ones, it's a blast. It gets a little messy what with mixing the rock salt and ice, but you'll get a few chuckles as everyone poops out trying to crank the machine until the frozen dessert is ready. Messy, hard work, but a delicious treat as everyone sits around eating, lamenting ice cream headaches and listening to the kids argue over who gets to lick the beaters. Now that's what I call old-fashioned family fun.

47. Attend an Unusual Sporting Event

How about fencing, polo, rugby, horseshoes, a rodeo, or the Special Olympics? This last one could be a double-event activity. Don't just go watch the Special Olympics, volunteer to be a helper/assistant/trainer. There's more to do than meets the eye. Quite often there's a need for drivers to and from the events, as well as serving food and cleaning up afterward.

48. Skip Rocks

Boy, here's one that will take you back to your childhood. Is there a dad among us who has never once skipped rocks? If so, let me enlighten you about this grand adventure. This can take two minutes, two hours, or an entire day, depending on the rocks, the weather, and your attitude. All you need is a body of water, large or small. When I say small, I mean small. It could be a puddle or a pond, a creek or a river, a leak or a lake. (If the body of water is really small, just make sure there are no people or windows on the other side.)

Look for rocks that are about the size of a silver dollar, as flat as possible, and, in a perfect rock-skipping world, shaped like a boomerang. I'll describe a right-handed toss; flip the directions over if you're left handed. Fold your bottom three fingers in toward your palm of your hand and grip the rock between your thumb and pointer finger, letting the rock rest on the bent fingers beneath it. Looking out across the body of water, take tree or four steps forward, bending slightly, and fling the rock toward the water in as low and straight a line as you can. The object here is for the stone to bounce on the water's surface as many times as possible. Three is fair, six is good, eight and up qualifies you for the U.S. Olympic rock-skipping trials in Yazoo, Mississippi.

When you take your kids out to do this, don't worry about sticking to my specific instructions. Use whatever approach works for you. Hold the rock as you wish, but make sure you teach your children as though you have been doing this all your life. It's a blast.

49. Design a Wind Chime

How difficult can this activity be? Have your child decide what makes the kind of sounds she would like to hear outside her bedroom window. Get some string and some pieces of metal, spoons and forks, bamboo, or anything else that you can think of that makes a pleasant sound. All you have to do is tie string, fishing line, or whatever you choose around your object of choice, each string a little longer than the first, to give the chime a nice spiral look. Some of your materials will need holes drilled in the top of them (like metal pipes or bamboo) to loop the string through.

After you have secured the strings to the individual chimes, make a loop at the top for your hanger. Find a spot to hang your creation where the wind blows softly, not in great gusts, so that the chime will tinkle you a tune rather than blow itself apart.

50. Take a Boating Excursion

There's usually a body of water within reach of everyone—a river, a lake, the ocean. Even if you don't own a boat or don't have a friend with a boat, you can always look into the possibility of getting someone to take you and your child out for a day of fishing or cruising. You can also rent smaller motorboats at many small lakes and lagoons. Call any marina listed in your yellow pages and chances are there is someone who captains sailboats or fishing boats for a hobby—or to earn a few extra bucks to help pay for his floating money pit.

Whatever type of boat you choose becomes a classroom for your child. Have him prepare a list of questions about how the boat operates. While he's on board, have him learn how to help cast off, cruise, and dock the boat when the day trip is over. If you have to pay for this pleasure trip, check to see if the rates are different for a half day. I took my son for an afternoon sail and discovered that not only was the afternoon trip less expensive, but we could actually sleep overnight on the boat if we were off by 7:00 the next morning. What a fun afternoon and fantastic night we had. It never hurts to ask.

51. Explore a Cave or a Mine

Every region has its own unusual geological areas. We have goldmines, but other areas have equally amazing sights to behold. We found a cave area in Iowa that had lush ferns equal to those in Hawaii and the area maintained a year-round temperature of 55 degrees—even while above ground there might be six feet of snow with a wind chill factor of 65 degrees below zero in the winter, or 100 degrees with 100 percent humidity in the summer. Look around your area. You'll be delighted with what you find.

If spelunking isn't your cup of dirt, go rock climbing with a guide, or try it first at a gym or exhibit where you can climb for five bucks. Rock climbing clubs are sprouting up everywhere. This is such a fun activity that we had a portable "rock" brought in to the remote area where our church held its annual girls' youth camp. The girls loved it, and so will your kids.

52. Play Sports Together

Doing this sharpens your child's athletic abilities—and it's an especially good way to get girls feeling good about themselves. This is most important for preteen and teen girls because it builds in them the confidence to compete with boys—and the knowledge that it's okay to do so. It's especially important because this is the age when a lot of girls lose their feelings of equality with boys.

Take your child to a batting cage, a driving range, or other similar sporting venue. Your local pro shop may even offer computerized analysis of what sports your child and you are best suited for, based on her build and body type.

Index

A

Activities. *See also* 52 quick ideas
American flag lesson, 237–242
for animal lovers, 88–91, 191–195
ball games, 170–175
bicycle riding lessons, 17–21
bicycle trips, 26–31
billiards, 143–149
bird watching, 108–111
board games, 150–155
bowling, 156–160
ceramics class, 161–164
cooking, 37–41
cooking contests, 225–228
dance lessons, 22–25
delittering, 104–107
dishwashing, 247–250
driving lessons, 133–138
family videos, 12–16, 274–275
fishing, 219–224
flying, 125–128
gardening, 243–246, 261–262
genealogy, 210–214
geography lesson, 118–124
Guinness World Records, 176–180
hamburger quest, 139–142
holiday traditions, 71–75, 205–209
horseback riding, 32–36
inventing a product, 181–185
jail time, 186–190
kid-friendly chores, 9
kite flying, 229–232
military facility tours, 165–169
motorcycle adventures, 92–96
music appreciation, 50–54
science projects, 42–45
service projects, 196–199, 205–209
sign language, 215–218
Sunday comics, 129–132
survivalist weekend, 82–87
tours, 60–65
train rides, 233–236
writing notes, 112–117
yo-yo tricks, 97–101
zoo day, 4–5, 6–7
Adventure Cycling, 30
Advice for dads
apologizing, 66–70
one-on-one time, 251–255
teaching respect, 76–81
teaching tolerance, 55–59
Albertson, Hal, 102–107
Alcatraz, 187–188
American flag, 237–242
American Kitefliers Association, 229–230, 231
American Yo-Yo Association, 98
Animals
endangered species, 279–280
horses, 32–36
pet care, 88–91, 191–195
Apologies, 66–70
Archeological dig, 267
Audubon Society, 109

B

Backyard campouts, 257–258
Ball games, 170–175
Bicycle
lessons, 17–21
trips, 26–31
Billiards, 143–149
Bird watching, 108–110
Birdhouses, 111
Birthday parties, 12–16
Board games, 150–155